DENISE LEOGRANDIS

Launching the Writing Workshop

A Step-by-Step Guide in Photographs

Foreword by Pam Allyn

SCHOLASTIC

New York • Toronto • London • Auckland • Sydney
Mexico City • New Delhi • Hong Kong • Buenos Aires

Acquisitions editor: Lois Bridges
Production editor: Jennifer DePrima
Cover design by Maria Lilja
Interior design by Holly Grundon
Interior photos by Denise Leograndis
Copy editor: David Klein

ISBN-13: 978-0-545-02121-0
ISBN-10: 0-545-02121-9

To my students—

Akul, Alani, Anslea, Ashley, Brandon, Brent, Brianna, Cesar, Christine, Francisco, Jaswant, Juan, Henry, Irma, Isaac, Isabella, Isaiah, Ivan, Marigrey, Marissa B., Marissa D., Martin, Mikayla, Moë, Noah, Rika, Shantal, and Yazmin

I am grateful for your help.

Contents

Foreword

Every teacher has spent time thinking about how to make the first weeks of school as exciting, productive, and meaningful as possible—especially when the start of school involves launching our writing workshop. There is so much to do, so little time, and we want to get it just right.

Once in a blue moon, a book comes along that answers *all* your questions about an important aspect of your teaching. This is one of those rare books.

Denise Leograndis knows exactly what we want to learn: how to structure the first four weeks of the year by putting together all the key pieces that support a great year of teaching writing.

The book is full of beautiful pictures of a classroom being transformed from its first-day state of readiness to its end-of-the-month richness, replete with charts, quotes, student work, and other striking visual imagery. Seeing is indeed believing, and the pictures Denise includes both exemplify and reinforce the points she is making in her writing. The visual images also provide a level of comfort—"What a great idea that is!"—and a level of excitement—"Wow, how magnificent that room looks as the students prepare to celebrate their writing!" Warm, inviting, and welcoming, Denise's book helps us breathe a sigh of relief and say, "I can do this!"

Denise's wise and wonderful voice leads us through the anxiety of those first days, when both we and our children are getting our "sea legs" and adjusting to the grade, to one another, and to the work at hand. Throughout the book, she maintains an essential focus on the underlying mission of creating a secure, comfortable environment for children to learn more about themselves as writers and the craft of writing.

In addition to her extraordinarily helpful and practical guidance on structure, content, and organization, Denise always keeps her eye on the main goal of instilling in our students from the very first day the understanding that writing is about conveying something meaningful and heartfelt to the reader. This constant emphasis on why we write and the power our words carry is the foundation beneath all the practical advice Denise gives us.

Deeply respectful of children as learners and storytellers, Denise has followed her own teaching and created a book that clearly speaks from her heart to ours. In her book Denise writes, "Readers have expectations. Writers have responsibilities." My expectation was that I would be reading a practical book on launching the writing workshop. My expectation was exceeded when I realized how genuinely Denise wants to give her students the power to create meaningful writing. And, for that act of taking a practical book and making it touch my heart, I hold her fully responsible. And I thank her. I hope this book gives you as much guidance and pleasure as it gave me.

—Pam Allyn

Acknowledgments

Many heartfelt thanks to:

My editor, Lois Bridges, who met me at an Italian café, slid Maria L. Chang's book *Classroom Management in Photographs* across the table, and suggested I do something similar—a book rich with photographs to help teachers.

Susan Hull, teacher, neighbor, and friend, who gave the start of my draft a first read one summer morning at my kitchen table, encouraged me to continue, and offered insightful feedback whenever I asked.

The dedicated teachers and literacy coaches at the Franklin–McKinley and Santa Clara Unified School Districts, for field-testing my draft—Alexis Redmond, Elizabeth DeVargas-Almeida, Jamie Lynn Lawrence, Janell Anderson, Janice Morse, Jenny Maehara, Kelly Mack, Leila Manning, Marie McEntee, Marilyn Armstrong, Paula Arnold, and Roy Bailey. Your enthusiastic comments and encouragement energized me.

Jenny Maehara, wonderful teacher in the classroom next door to me, for your daily support and encouragement, and for taking the photo with me in it.

My students and their families of the 2007–2008 school year, who gladly gave permission for photos and writing samples. I could not have done this work without you.

And last, but probably most, many thanks to my family for your technical and emotional support, especially as my deadline approached and I was holed up in my office for hours and days on end. You're the best.

Introduction

For this book I have taken a camera into my classroom and photographed every element of my writing workshop launch—the room, the mentor texts, students in action, and mostly, the charts. I know from teaching teachers over the past seven years that seeing what charts might look like is so helpful. Every learner, including teachers, needs visuals.

This book will take you from the days before the first bell through the first four weeks of school. Through text and photos you will see how to establish a positive and productive writing workshop with clear expectations. You will learn to build for your students a foundational understanding and appreciation of literature while you create the start of a successful school year.

I love the launch. I love the anticipation, the excitement, the promise of it all. The promise that this year will be even better than the last. That my new group of students and I will soon meld into one solid learning adventure team. I don't hold back my smile until December—it's out from the first minute on the first day. I'm excited! How could I not smile? Welcome, I say. Welcome to our wonderful place of learning. Feel safe. Feel empowered. Let's get started.

Terms and Definitions

craft: A broad term, both a noun and a verb, that covers everything a writer does to construct and create wonderfully readable writing. Writers practice their craft and craft their writing much like musicians, artists, and actors do.

genre: A category of artistic, musical, or literary composition characterized by a particular style, form, or content (from Merriam-Webster's Collegiate Dictionary, 10th ed., 2000).

immersion: Immersing your class in read-alouds, to get your students thinking about and absorbing the features of a particular writing genre. The "What is it?"

inquiry: Close study of writing to think about and understand how a writer crafts the text. The "How is it done?"

long-write: Writing done in the writer's notebook, with no intent to write a finished piece, although a draft could be based on all or part of a long-write. The writer chooses an idea or a memory or a topic and simply writes a lot about it.

mentor text: Any writing studied in order to understand writers' craft, with the intent of improving one's own writing.

mini-lesson structure: A lesson modified from a traditional structure to fit the "mini" time frame and to serve the ongoing work in a workshop. See Appendix B for a black-line master.

pacing: The flow of the writing; the rate at which the reader is moved through the text. This will vary according to the mood of the text and the writer's purpose.

seed idea: The genesis or source of a piece of writing.

unit of study: A time period of one to six weeks, but typically three to four weeks, when the workshop is focused on studying one genre, or writers' processes, or craft elements across genres.

Before You Begin

Goals

- Build a safe writing community

- Establish rituals and routines

- Generate lots of thinking, talk and writing

- Develop the understanding that all good writing has meaning, detail, structure and pacing

The Big Picture

Of course you will modify the pace, level of language, and content of this launch unit in any way you see fit. Whatever modifications you decide upon, remember that the purpose of the launch is to establish a classroom writing community, a place where students feel safe to share the personal moments and passionate pursuits they are just beginning to learn to express in writing. This is no easy task for you, the teacher. You have a room full of individual personalities to bring together into one literature-loving unit. The good news is, when you express your love, passion, and fascination for literature and for the writing process, you provide a model so powerful your students can't help but join you on this journey of discovery.

The Four-Week Launch

- **Week 1.** Establish rituals and routines, introduce the writer's notebook, and begin collecting a variety of meaningful entries.

- **Week 2.** Focus on purposeful sensory detail, introduce pacing in writing.

- **Week 3.** Focus on choosing and developing one idea to take through the writing process.

- **Week 4.** Complete the writing process, reflect, and celebrate.

The Charts

The photographs show the launch charts in my third- and fourth-grade combo class for the year I am writing this book. The charts are meant to be a guide for you to adjust to your grade level and classroom and to the ideas of your own students. When you ask for and record your own students' responses, remember there are no right or wrong answers, only ideas that make sense.

The Tone of the Workshop

What I can't show you in photographs is the tone of the workshop. Your voice should always convey a tone of respect and passion for writing and a writer's work.

Read-Alouds and Your Writing Work

During these first weeks of school you'll need to read a lot of quality age-appropriate illustrated books across genres, including poetry. You and your students will first enjoy and respond to the literature as readers and then later come back to the familiar text as writers in writing workshop mini-lessons. Aside from the first day, you don't want to take time in your writing workshop to read an entire book.

After a read-aloud, I pause, give some wait time, and then ask students to turn and talk about what they just heard. First, to honor their individual responses as readers, anything goes. Next, direct their thinking by asking questions that will support the work in your writing workshop. I can give you suggestions for those questions.

The caption "Books to Enjoy Today as First Reads" means that the books mentioned should be read sometime during your day. That way, the text will be familiar when you use it the next day as a mentor text in your writing workshop. If you substitute a book with a choice of your own, make sure it will work in the intended mini-lesson.

Reading Workshop and Your Writing Work

During the first month of school, I am establishing rituals and routines in my reading workshop, assessing reading levels, celebrating literature by reading, sharing, and talking about books, and guiding students to find "just-right" books on their own. After establishing book-selection processes and workshop routines, my reading workshop mini-lessons will begin to connect to our writing work. For instance, during Week 2 of the writing workshop launch, we are working to add sensory detail to our writing. So in the reading workshop, I'll start work on the comprehension strategy of visualizing while reading, and have students mark their independent reading chapter books with sticky notes when they find sensory detail that supports their visualizing.

Informal Author Study

Because you will be teaching the writing process, I recommend choosing one grade-level-appropriate author to focus on. You can record on chart paper and/or discuss what you learn about him or her through the author's Web site or books. Author interviews on http://

www.scholastic.com are another helpful resource. You will find printed and video interviews there. Whomever you choose, read a lot of your chosen author's works, discuss the author's topic choices and genre choices, and research your author's writing process. When you study the writing life of an author, your students will connect their own developing writing lives to the work and processes of published writers. It's the same as connecting your student's developing work and processes as a scientist to that of a practicing scientist. It makes the work more exciting, engaging, and meaningful. You'll see I have chosen Jane Yolen for this launch. Her collection of work is so varied and her Web site is full of information about her work and processes.

Language Use and Conventions and Your Writing Work

I use grade-level standards and formal and informal assessments of my students' writing work to decide what to teach in my Language Use and Conventions block. During the first month of school, to support my writing workshop launch, I will use that half-hour block of time to study ending punctuation, capitalization, and spelling rules and strategies. Every morning students use what they are learning in a self-edit of their writing homework. For further reading on improving your students' spelling, I recommend Cindy Marten's (2003) *Word Crafting: Teaching Spelling, Grades K–6*. For further reading on conventions work, see Janet Angelillo's (2002) *A Fresh Approach to Teaching Punctuation*.

Writing Homework and Your Writing Work

Students need extended practice, particularly in writing. It is such a difficult skill to develop. At the end of each day, I'll post a Try-It or a Do-It on the board to give students an idea of what to write at home. Before they go home, we chant and pantomime "write, write, write, backpack." If their backpacks make it back to school, and they always do, their notebook will as well.

First thing the next morning, have a homework check and notebook share for five to ten minutes. The notebook share can be a powerful tool to move your writers forward. As you move around the room checking homework, have students share their writing with the person next to them, and talk about their decisions behind what they wrote. Share struggles and success. Share how the writing homework got done; how did they find the time, place, and discipline to write? Talk about how it feels to write meaningful entries. Choose a few students to share out to the whole group. Better yet, ask students to nominate their partner to share out his or her writing homework and explain why. Keep track of who has shared his or her writing or process to be sure that over time everyone shares.

After the share, students should edit their writing for conventions they already know and/ or those you have taught so far. You want them to develop an editing habit, not save editing for one day in the writing process. If a student somehow forgot his or her notebook on the previous day and didn't think to find any piece of paper to write on, I look completely stunned and incredulous. I ask the student how he or she plans to remember to bring the notebook from here on out. (The chanting pantomime at the end of the day would be a good cue.) Then I inform the class that, should they ever be in such a pickle, any piece of paper will do, and it can be taped into their notebooks at the first chance. I show them how I had to do just that one time when I went camping and forgot my notebook.

Adjusting the Launch for Yourself, Your Class, and Grade Level

There is a wiggle-room day built into each of the first two weeks. You may find you need to spend more time on a concept, or two days on one lesson, or you may lose a day to an assembly or to Labor Day. Some lessons and more abstract concepts, such as the "Digging Deeper" lesson of Day 3, may not be developmentally appropriate for younger learners. You should adjust the level of the language in the scripted lessons to your grade level. You know your students best and can make the best decisions on what needs tweaking, and when.

Language Learners

Technically, all your students are learning English. There are currently 23 languages spoken at my school. Our students have the full range of English acquisition, including English language learners with stronger English than some English-only students. This year, 12 of my students are English learners. In your writing workshop, students with little or no English should begin the school year writing in their own language. It is most important to get their thoughts down. They will gradually insert and then substitute English. Be sure to provide mentor text examples at accessible levels for all your students, especially in the second week, with the focus on sensory detail. This year a boy from Russia mixed drawings with the writing in his notebook to express himself when he did not have the words. My Spanish-speaking student gets daily help with translation from my bilingual students. One girl from Japan gets extra editing assistance from me with her articles and plurals. I have enlisted parents as translators for the new-to-our-country students. Every child is different. Through deep immersion into the structure and meaning of text, and through lots of writing practice, every child makes remarkable progress in a well-run writing workshop.

Mentor Text With Matching Teaching Point List

When I first started teaching, I tracked down lists of mentor texts and simply bought every book on the lists. What a mistake! You need to find books you like to teach from and that are grade-level appropriate. If you love and/or are fascinated by the text, your students will be as well. I recommend you borrow the texts on this list from your library and then buy only the ones you fall in love with. Some of these will go out of print with time. But you can easily and inexpensively buy used books, typically library discards, from sellers on the Internet. And, of course, keep on the lookout for wonderful, newly published books and share your finds with other teachers.

These books vary in complexity and sophistication. In some, the illustrations give more information to the reader to support comprehension, while in other illustrated books the text can stand on its own and the level of the text can be quite sophisticated. Either way, they are short compared to a chapter book or novel. We are asking our student writers to write short texts, and in younger grades, to illustrate and write short texts. Therefore we need to use the structure of short texts as models and mentors.

This list is organized by teaching points and the books that support those teaching points. That means, with the exception of Day 1, you need to read the books to your class at least once just for enjoyment, outside of writing workshop and *before* the mini-lesson. At least one day before is best. You can substitute your own mentor text choices, but be sure they will support the matching lesson's teaching point.

Day 1
Teaching point: Writers get ideas of what to write about from books.

- *My Very Own Room* (Spanish and English) by Amada Irma Pérez

Day 2
Teaching point: Writers get ideas of what to write about from objects. Choose one or two:

- *What You Know First* by Patricia MacLachlan
- *A Chair for My Mother* (also in Spanish) by Vera B. Williams
- *Wilfrid Gordon McDonald Partridge* by Mem Fox
- *William's Doll* by Charlotte Zolotow

Day 3
Teaching point: Writers think deeply to find the meaning of their writing.

- *When I Was Young in the Mountains* by Cynthia Rylant
- *My Rotten Redheaded Older Brother* by Patricia Polacco

Day 4
Teaching point: Writers draw and sketch to find meaningful ideas to write about. Writers write from the heart and in many different genres.

- *How Do Dinosaurs Say Goodnight?* by Jane Yolen (or any book in this series)
- *Welcome to the Greenhouse* by Jane Yolen

Day 5

Wiggle-room day.

Day 6

Teaching point: Writers use sensory detail to draw in the reader; focus on sound.

- *Owl Moon* by Jane Yolen

- *Night in the Country* by Cynthia Rylant

Day 7

Teaching point: Writers use sensory detail to draw in the reader; focus on touch.

- *Owl Moon* by Jane Yolen

- *My Father's Hands* by Joanne Ryder

Day 8

Teaching point: Writers use sensory detail to draw in the reader; focus on sight.

- *Owl Moon* by Jane Yolen

- "Gimmetheball" from *Rimshots* by Charles R. Smith, Jr.

Day 9

Teaching point: Writers use sensory detail to draw in the reader; focus on smell.

- *Come On, Rain!* by Karen Hesse

- *Oma's Quilt* by Paulette Bourgeois

- *Henry and Mudge: The First Book* by Cynthia Rylant

Day 10

This is a wiggle-room day, with an option for studying how sensory details related to taste are used in writing. Use age-appropriate cookbooks.

Days 11–20

You will be completing the writing process and referring back to previously read books.

Before the Start of School
Getting Ready

Use this set of photos as a checklist to set up your room for the writing workshop.

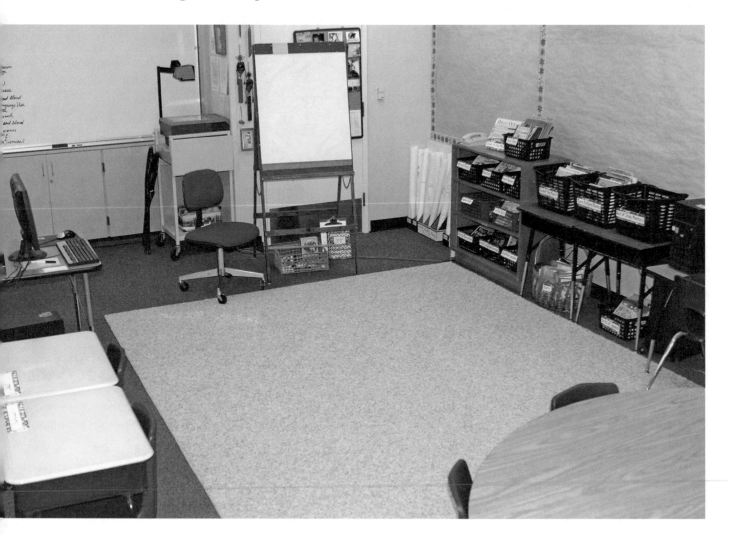

P.1 | Meeting Area

You'll need to arrange your room so that there is a sitting-on-the-carpet meeting area. The meeting area is a place where you and your students will leave the individual and separate spaces that chairs and desks define and become one on the carpet. The intimacy and purpose of your work together as writers is physically represented by your closeness.

P.2 | Easel

At the meeting area, you'll be in a chair or on a stool next to an easel with chart paper. Have your easel high enough so all students can see over the heads in front of them to the bottom of the chart paper.

P.3 | Teacher Supplies

Have your teacher supplies nearby; a basket near the easel will work. You will need these items: colored markers, sticky notes, 1″ correction tape, correction fluid, clear tape for repairing tears, highlighter markers, and a pencil and colored sharpies for marking photocopies of mentor texts. A dictionary is handy as well;

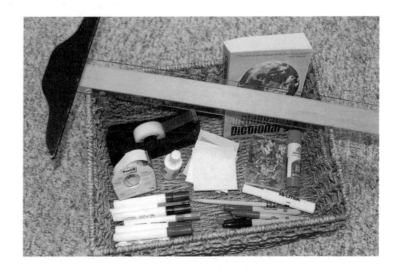

I model using the same one my students have. That orange-topped glue stick in the basket is repositionable glue—it turns your charts and papers into instant giant sticky notes so you can easily reposition charts on the wall and back and forth from your easel. I will use pushpins to keep a stack of charts secure on my chart wall. A T-square is useful for making straight vertical and horizontal lines on your charts.

P.4 | Seating

Desk arrangement should allow and encourage talk. I have always had group seating—two students facing two students, in clusters of four. However, this year I am using an LCD projector with my computer for the first time, in all my different curricular areas. My students let me know the clusters of four weren't working. They chose this seating arrangement, front facing and in rows, to allow for easy viewing, but shoulder-to-shoulder for talking with neighbors. In writing workshops I draft, revise, and edit in front of my students on the big screen. I can type fast, and they can see and hear my thinking, and read my writing. My fast writing on chart paper on the easel is too messy. They move themselves to carpet areas for peer conferring groups. When group deskwork is required, rows are transformed back into clusters of four with some quick turns of desks. You'll need to decide what will work best for you and your students.

P.5 | Conferring Chair

You will need a chair for conferring. I like this inexpensive model—it folds and unfolds so I can easily move around the room and pull up next to students. Sitting next to your students to confer, rather than calling them to you, honors their work and their processes as writers.

P.6 | Group Conference Table

Conferring happens in small groups as well as in individual conferences. You could get on the floor with a small group, but I prefer a table where we can spread out and I can still monitor the rest of the room from my position in the corner.

P.7 | Conferring Clipboard and Conference Top Sheet

I use this quick visual to make sure I am attending equally to every student and not over- or under-conferring with any one student. I keep this sheet on top of my assessment sheets on this clipboard. As I confer with a child, I put a letter in the box to indicate where he or she is in the writing process: C for collect, P for plan, D for draft, and so on. The letter notation will keep me from accidentally conferring with a child during only one part of the writing process.

P.8 | Conference Assessment Sheet

This is an informal assessment sheet I use to start gathering data about my students' strengths and areas of needed improvement. (See Appendix D for a reproducible version of this sheet.) After a conference, I'll make notes under "What's done well," "What's needed," and "Conventions." I immediately use the data gathered under Conventions to plan lessons for my Language Use and Conventions daily half-hour. Student's names are not in alphabetical order because before school starts I begin to think about grouping the students for future small-group work and group conferences. I look at their language-learner levels, individualized education plans, 504s, and the writing in their portfolios from the previous school year. For my units after the launch, I add a more precise assessment sheet based on our genre grade-level standards. For more on assessment, see Carl Anderson's (2005) *Assessing Writers*.

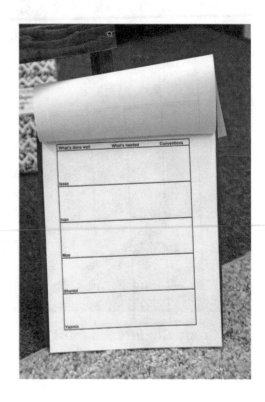

P.9 | Chart Display

The purpose of charts and a chart display area is to capture and show the work of your launch, and subsequent units of study, so students can independently access and re-access the information. This is the longest wall in my room, divided into three sections: Reading Workshop, Writing Workshop, and Language Use and Conventions—the three inseparable parts of the literacy curriculum.

P.10 | Chart Storage: Stacking

If your unit is in progress but you're running out of space, do a quick chart walk where you ask students which charts they need and which can be covered but still be available. Then stack a few charts using pushpins. Students can easily lift charts to see the one underneath if they still need to access that information.

P.11 | Chart Storage: Hangers

You can choose to store your charts, grouped together in units of study, on hangers.

P.12 | Chart Storage: Binders

You can choose to photograph your charts and store them in a single binder that students can access, or photocopy the pages for students to keep in their writing folders. If you're shooting with a digital camera, store photos as computer files instead of having them printed.

P.13 | Chart Storage: Storage Boxes

For charts I know I'll be reusing, I like this space-saver system.

P.14 | Writers' Supplies: Whole Class

Designate an area where your student writers can find the supplies they need: newsprint (for galley books), yellow draft paper, lined paper for publishing, pencils, blue editing pencils or pens, tape, staplers, sticky notes, scissors, clipboards, dictionaries, thesauruses, and books on grammar and style.

In one drawer are red and green tags, cut from construction paper. These can be used to serve as a signaling system—a child who puts out a green tag on his or her desk is requesting a teacher conference. A child with a red tag does not want to stop writing for a teacher conference. See the chart and more information on page 50, photo 3.4.

P.15 | Supplies for Individual Students

Writer's notebooks await each student on the first day of school, along with folders for different curricular areas. Students need to develop good habits of organization. A personal writing folder is a place where a student can keep all items for one writing project—drafts, editing sheet, photocopied pages of mentor texts. I use inexpensive pocket folders in purple, which look good with yellow draft paper. We use "Quick-Word" as a spelling resource for high-frequency words.

P.16 | Portfolio and Draft Storage

Students should have easy access to their writing portfolios, where they store and thoughtfully update examples of their best finished pieces. I designate a filing cabinet drawer and have an additional file for each student, behind the portfolio files, where they can store old drafts and other writing work to keep their purple writing folders from overflowing.

P.17 | Unit of Study Mentor Basket

This basket should be empty on the first day of school. You will be reading books to your students over the course of the launch unit that you and your students will want to refer back to without having to search all around your room for them. In this launch unit and all your subsequent units of study, this basket will serve as a single, easily accessible place to hold your mentor texts.

P.18 | Access to Mentor Texts

Whether you check out stacks of books from your library or you have amassed your own collection, you will need to organize them so students have quick and easy access. I prefer to organize by author.

P.19 | Writing Process Wheel

I keep this up all year, taped to my white board. It's a quick check for me to see where everyone is in any one unit of study. Students' names are on magnet strips. I instruct students to move their own names around the wheel, and I tell them that they may sometimes need to go counterclockwise as well as clockwise. Explain to your students, in language they'll understand, that the reason all sections of this chart touch in the middle is because the writing process is recursive, not linear. For the first day of school, all names are in "Collect," because that is where we will all be starting. Make yourself part of your writing community by including your own name.

Week 1

Collecting Meaningful Entries
in the Writer's Notebook

Four Goals

- Begin to build a safe and productive writing community

- Establish rituals and routines

- Develop the understanding that writing has meaning

- Generate lots of thinking, talk, and writing

Overview of Week 1

The focus of this first week is on meaning, because the first thing writers do before crafting their writing is to have or find something to say . . . something meaningful, important, significant, heartfelt that the writer wishes to communicate to the reader. This week, you want your students to begin learning what the process of discovery feels like. Some writers come to understand what they are trying to say after talking through ideas with others, some through quiet contemplation, and many through the act of writing itself. When you begin your year with this heavy focus on meaning, you set the stage for success throughout the year, helping your student writers avoid bed-to-bed personal narratives, empty poetry, rambling fiction, and pointless expository writing. When you further support this focus on meaning in your reading work, you will nurture strong writers and readers.

A Note About Meaningful Writing

Meaning for our student writers has a developmentally appropriate lens. As teachers, we will enjoy and honor heartfelt meaning at our grade levels of understanding and articulation while keeping our expectations high and encouraging all students to be thoughtful writers.

The Tone of the Workshop

Remember to have in your voice a tone of respect and passion for writing and a writer's work.

Adjusting the Week for Yourself, Your Class, and Grade Level

There is a wiggle-room day built into this week. Beginning-of-the-year assemblies may eat one of your days. Or you may find you need to spend more time on a concept. And if you are teaching third grade or below, you'll likely find you need two days for Day 1.

Suggestions for Supporting Work to Do in Your Reading Workshop

Choose an author to begin an informal author study. I have written this launch with Jane Yolen as our focus author because her work is broad and varied across genres and audiences and there is so much information on her Web site.

Supporting Work to Do in Your Language Use and Conventions Block

Assess your students' writing for conventions and spelling. Check your grade-level standards and begin to teach what they need. Beginning this week, preferably by Day 3, have students self-edit their writing homework every morning; you will want to model this initially. You can use a piece of your own writing that you create for this purpose, or ask a student for permission to make copies or an overhead transparency of a page of his or her work.

Supporting Daily Homework and Homework Share

Except for the first day of school, my students write every night as part of their daily homework. I tell them, "The more you practice, the better you get, as in anything you do in your life."

The Try-It is tied to the day's work. However, the Try-It is not a Do-It because this week I also want to leave the option open for students to be free to do any kind of writing they are inspired to do. Explain to your students that the Try-It is optional. They may write whatever they like, they may get a new idea not on their jot list, but they should be prepared to explain the next day why what they wrote about is meaningful to them.

We will chant and pantomime "write, write, write, backpack" every day until it looks like they have internalized it. You can add "read, read, read, backpack" if you'd like, to encourage your students to bring the same book back and forth until it's finished.

Tell them that tomorrow and every morning for the rest of the school year, first thing, they will have their notebooks out and open on their desks to read to the person next to them (and for you to read), and you will ask a few students to share.

Introducing the
Writer's Notebook

Overview

Y
ou cannot cover every ritual and routine you need for a smoothly running writing workshop in one day, so on the first day cover the essentials. Your community-building will start today with lots and lots of sharing and talk. Most important, through everything you say and do and the way you say and do it, your big goal today and throughout the year is to celebrate literature for what it is—meaningful, powerful, essential, and basic to the quality of the human experience.

1.1 | Chart Walls

There are no charts before you begin your first workshop on this first day, because you have not taught or explored anything yet (see p. 21, photo P.9).

Supplies

Some time before your writing workshop begins, go over your expectations for using and storing individual student supplies (see p. 24, photo P.15). I have my students use fine-point permanent markers to write their names on their supplies. Giving them time to explore "Quick-Word" will increase the likelihood that they will actually use it daily as a resource.

1.2 | Books to Enjoy Today as First Reads

I don't read all of these today, but I do read a lot to my students throughout the first day of school, usually two or three selections. It's a comfortable, welcoming first-day thing to do, and we begin to learn about

each other through the talk and sharing that follow each reading. In addition, any of these four books will set up tomorrow's mini-lesson about how an object can unlock a story or spark an idea.

I like *What You Know First* by Patricia MacLachlan because many children have moved. They connect with the story. We come back to it in later units as writers to study the gorgeous language.

I use *A Chair for My Mother* by Vera B. Williams because of the focus on family, for it is with family whom the students have spent all summer until today. We come back to it later as writers when we study possibilities for narrative structure. I welcome my Spanish readers and speakers with a copy in Spanish that they can enjoy on their own.

William's Doll by Charlotte Zolotow is a wonderful beginning-of-the-year book on so many levels. We spend time on the first day talking about the book's theme of acceptance and how we are all individuals. It's part of the groundwork I do to create class rules, which include being kind. I like to come back to *William's Doll* in later language-study units when we are exploring the structure and purpose of really, really long sentences.

Wilfrid Gordon McDonald Partridge by Mem Fox is fun and meaningful for any age group, with an accessible level of language for younger students.

1.3 | Beginning to Explore Meaning

You can start this chart today, or over the next few days. After you enjoy a read-aloud, allow students time to think about why the writer wrote the book—why it was meaningful to the writer. Why is it meaningful to us? You can record all or some of your discussions. You'll guess at the author's meaning unless you can find the answer in an author interview somewhere. But this is important work to help support the thinking behind the topic choices your students will be making as writers. I keep this chart posted on my reading workshop chart wall (see photo 2.1).

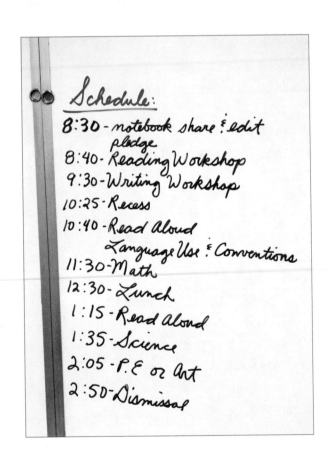

Writing Has Meaning

Title & Author	Possible Meaning for Author	Meaning for Us
What You Know First by Patricia MacLachlan	She loved the prairie so much. (She still carries a bag of prairie dirt.)	We know the pain of moving, of leaving a place you know & love.
William's Doll by Charlotte Zolotow	We think she had a similar experience. She wanted a basketball	We know what it is like to be teased. We know what it is like to feel different
My Very Own Room by Amada Irma Pérez	She loves her family and they support her.	Wanting something badly. Sleeping in crowded place. Special to be with family.

Schedule:
8:30 - notebook share & edit pledge
8:40 - Reading Workshop
9:30 - Writing Workshop
10:25 - Recess
10:40 - Read Aloud Language Use & Conventions
11:30 - Math
12:30 - Lunch
1:15 - Read Aloud
1:35 - Science
2:05 - P.E or Art
2:50 - Dismissal

1.4 | The Workshop Time: Make it Predictable

This is a typical day's schedule after the first day of school; we are obviously not sharing writing homework in our notebooks first thing on the first day. Following a predictable daily routine and schedule helps your students to habitually switch from reader to writer to mathematician to scientist, therefore maximizing their concentration and efforts in each curricular area.

Call your students to the carpet at the same time, the same way every day. I say, "It's time for writing workshop—please come to the carpet." I may add, "With your writer's notebook and a pencil" or "With your draft," if that is what is necessary for that day's mini-lesson. On this first day, direct them to bring their new writer's notebooks and a pencil—and be sure to have yours at the ready.

1.5 | Sitting on the Carpet

Have your students sit with absolute attention to you and your lesson. There is no time to waste. You can decide to assign spots or have students choose. On this first day, since they have their notebooks, decide whether they will be holding them in their laps, or placing the notebooks in front of them. Sitting on them seems disrespectful, and the notebooks' spines could break. You decide what is age-appropriate and what sort of management you prefer. When I see everyone is sitting on the carpet, my last signal before beginning the mini-lesson is verbal: "Check yourself." I teach students that this signal means check that you are facing me, sitting with your legs crossed, not touching anyone, or fiddling with anything. If I see this coming-to-the-carpet routine is not done quickly and smoothly, I have my students return to their seats, and we do it again.

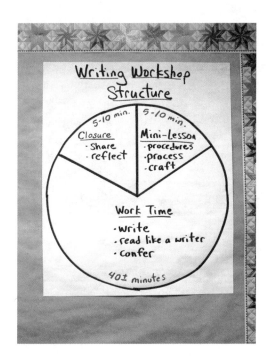

1.6 | The Pie Chart

Make a choice here. You can hold off introducing this chart until tomorrow, because your workshop won't follow the chart today. So today or tomorrow, after "check yourself," show this premade chart. Explain that writing workshop will be happening at this same time every day throughout the entire school year. Tell them this predictable and daily time will allow them to sustain their thoughts and efforts in their writing projects—it's what writers do. Sometimes the mini-lesson part may be longer, and because you are all just getting to know each other, this first day is one of those days. Tell them you'll put the pie chart on the writing wall, and it will stay there until everyone has internalized it.

1.7 | Introducing the Writer's Notebook

Hold up one of their new, empty writer's notebooks and your own worn, full, and possibly decorated one. (If you don't have your own notebook, don't worry—take an extra student issue and make it your own.) Explain that the writer's notebook is a very special, essential writer's tool. It is a place for capturing ideas, thoughts, and memories that are meaningful to the

writer. Repeat—*meaningful to the writer*. Today, this first day of school, they will begin to fill their writer's notebooks with entries that are meaningful to them.

1.8 | The Loosely Structured First Mini-Lesson

Teaching point: Writers get ideas of what to write about from books. Under your pie chart, have this "A Writer's Notebook" chart made and ready to go. Depending on your grade level, this one chart could be three charts, in larger print, but I like to consolidate, and the sections help students compare and contrast the different elements of their writer's notebooks.

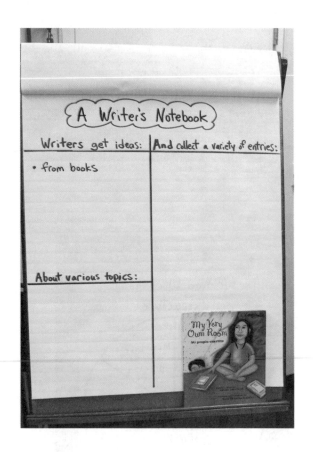

Have a book ready to read that your students can connect to, one that is written in first person and is about everyday life (so your students will understand that writing stories of their lives doesn't mean a blow-by-blow of their last trip to an amusement park). I like *My Very Own Room* by Amada Irma Pérez. I have found that everyone connects to at least one part of this book in some way. Be sure to share the back page, where the teacher/writer shares a bit about her life and family.

Explain: Flip to this Writer's Notebook chart and tell your students that writers often get ideas of what to write about from their own reading lives. That's what they'll be doing today. Tell them, "Now we'll enjoy this story, and when I am finished reading, we will talk about stories of our own lives that this story has unlocked."

1.9 | Thinking and Talking Before Writing

When you finish reading, first ask students just to think about sharing what this book reminded them of in their own lives. Give some wait time, and then model your own story. Next, have them turn and share with the person next to them, before you call on a few to share with the group. Be encouraging, be patient; there is a level of shyness on the first day of school, so this might go quite slowly.

> ## Jot Page
>
> - My cousin sleeps crazy
> - going to the tree house
> - My aunt Mavel

1.10 | Using the Notebook, the Jot Page

Once a few stories are rolling, briefly model getting an idea from a student (unless another student beats you to it) and write "from listening to others" under "from books." Then say, "We have started getting so many memories, if we don't write them down, we may lose them!" Write "Jots" in the "Variety of Entries" section on your chart. Model finding a page near the back of your notebook, and writing "Jot Page" on the top. Have all students do the same. Then model writing your own jots and explain that a jot is not a complete sentence, just enough to capture a memory, thought, or idea. Remember, your modeling is a very powerful tool; model all possibilities so you don't inadvertently shut down any thinking. Model writing a jot that seems directly related to the book, one more tangential, and one triggered by what another student has to say. Now have your students do the same. You can easily keep going here to the end of your writing workshop time, with stories triggering stories, and lots of talking, sharing, and jotting, but you'll want to save some time for "writing long" off a jot.

Note for younger grades: Make a decision here based on your time and your students' needs. After students have a list of jots started, the next piece to teach is that writers write long off chosen jots. But how is your time going on this first day? Younger children take at least twice as long as older children just to write the words "Jot Page." If your jotting and sharing uses the entire workshop time, you can start your workshop at this point tomorrow. I usually make time to write long after the recess break that follows our writing workshop because my students typically come back from recess begging to have more time to write. On this first day, I am going to follow that passion rather than a set time to end the workshop. However it works for you, today or tomorrow, writing long is the next piece after jotting.

1.11 | **Writing Long**

After all students have at least two jots, model the process of choosing one to write more about. Mention how important all these memories are to you, so it is hard to choose, but one seems to be tugging at you more than the others right now. Be clear that you will likely write long off of all your jots at some point. And that you are so happy to have this jot list of important memories started that you can add to at any time and refer to at any time for an idea to write about. Now model how to make notebook entries: on the right side, leaving the page on the left side blank, date and title at the top, skipping lines. Excuse them to write long.

   Link and excuse to write: Link the work they will be doing during independent writing time to what you expect in closure. Tell them that after independent writing time, you will gather for about ten minutes, and they will choose to share either the *process* of how they chose which jot to write long off of, or their *product*—their long write. Write with your students. You are a fast adult. Five minutes should be enough. It doesn't have to be good writing. They need to see you writing, and you need to be able to share your processes and your results at closure. You are the leader. Your modeling and your writing will energize your students, and you will be energized as well.

8-28-07

grandma's house
One day Gabe, My little Brother
and I whent to my grandmas
house, My dad drove us te her house
When we got ther we Play For
a little Bet. Then, It. Was time for
Bed. We made a big bed on the
Flor. My Brother's had ther Feet
on my Feet. it Felt like it
Was croaed.

1.12 | Mid-Workshop Teach: Rereading Strategy

After you and your students have written a bit, and you are now walking around the room looking over students' shoulders and smiling and nodding as they continue to write, you may notice some students have finished writing. Teach them how to keep going. Say, "Excuse me, writers, I notice some of you have finished writing long off your jot. When this happens to you and there is still independent writing time left in our workshop, then you have some choices. You can reread what you've just written. [*Briefly model this.*] Rereading helps a writer remember more details, and you can add more to this entry. Or rereading may trigger new important memories and ideas that you can add to your jot page. Or, you can go back to your jot page and choose a new jot and start a new entry on a new page."

1.13 | Closure

After all the reading, jotting, talking, and writing, your students will be excited to share what they've written and hear what others have written. You will always want to tie your closure back to the mini-lesson and focus on more learning about either the process or the product of the day's work. For this closure, I prefer to leave it open to process or product, whichever a student feels compelled to share, because the sharing itself is the main goal. Call your students back to the carpet meeting area and have them share with each other. You should also share with a student near you. Then have the group sit around the perimeter of your meeting area and ask for volunteers to share out to the group. As the sharing proceeds, record the topics that come up on the Writer's Notebook chart so your students can see that in their developing community they have so much in common; they have chosen to write about similar meaningful topics—family, friends, pets, and similar events (see photo 2.4). Point out these similarities and use the word "meaningful" a lot. Be sure to share your writing and enthusiasm with the group.

1.14 | Writers' Homework

Starting tomorrow, I'll have a Try-It on the whiteboard, a suggestion to write an entry that is tied to the day's work, but for tonight I ask students to spend some time as writers, thoughtfully looking around their home for special objects or photographs that have great meaning for them: something that triggers a meaningful story or memory, something they'll

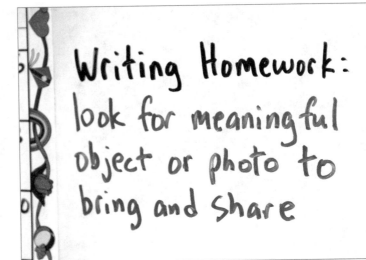

bring tomorrow to share, talk about, and write about. At this point I'll also introduce the writing process wheel, as it is right there on my whiteboard next to the Try-It (see photo P.19). All their names and my name are in "Collect." I'll explain that we are starting the writing process by collecting entries and ideas in our notebooks, and we'll be doing that for the next two weeks.

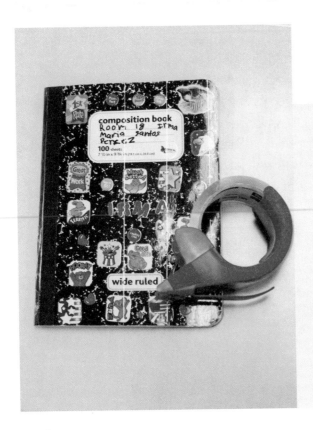

1.15 | Decorating Notebooks

Sometime soon, you'll want to give your students a chance to decorate their notebooks, to personalize them and make them special instead of generic. You can provide stickers or ask students to donate stickers, or bring in photos for their own notebooks, or whatever other creative idea you or they may have. I use postal tape to secure, seal, and strengthen their decorated notebooks.

Getting More Meaningful
Ideas to Write About

Remember your tone—it is infectious, so share your respect and passion for literature, for writing, and for a writer's work.

Overview

Today you'll review and reinforce routines as needed from yesterday—adding new routines, continuing to build community, and emphasizing your ongoing focus on meaning. On this second day, and for the rest of your launch, your mini-lesson will follow a standard sequence (connect, teach/model, turn and talk/practice, link, closure), unlike yesterday, where you spent a big chunk of time reading an entire book. From now on, read an entire book during your designated read-aloud times, outside of the writing workshop hour, allowing your students to respond to and enjoy the writing first as readers. Then later, in your writing mini-lessons, you'll take your students back to parts of the book and study the text as writers.

If you are continuing your lesson from yesterday because you ran long, you will open your lesson with a Connect and Teach that sounds something like, "Writers, yesterday we learned that writers capture, keep, and continually add to a running list of jots so they have something to write from in their writers' notebooks. Today, you'll be doing what writers do and writing long off one of your jots." Then continue from the Long Write on Day 1, and this Day 2 will become Day 3.

Some time today, go over your expectations for accessing and using the classroom writers' supplies (see photo P.15).

2.1 | Chart Walls

My writing and reading chart walls look like this after my first day and before starting my second day.

2.2 | Books to Enjoy Today as First Reads

My Rotten Redheaded Older Brother by Patricia Polacco and *When I Was Young in the Mountains* by Cynthia Rylant are memoirs in which the writers added an obvious reflection to tell the reader why the writing is meaningful for them. You can add these obvious reflections to your Writing Has Meaning chart. Also remember to model adding to your jot page in your notebook; add an idea or memory that comes to you after a read-aloud and/or discussion. Give students a minute or two to do the same. When students maintain a running jot list, you should never hear, "I don't know what to write about." As you revisit and model the jot strategy daily, you are giving your students a chance to internalize it and develop their identities as writers.

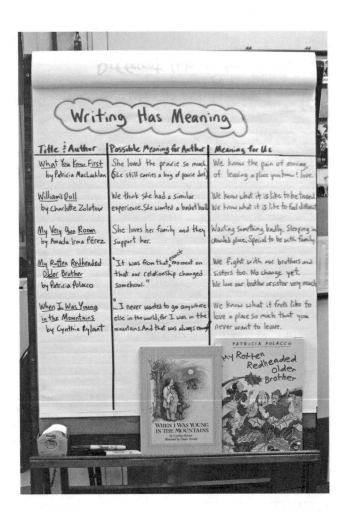

2.3 | Author Support

Above my literacy chart walls, I post author quotes that support teaching points and strengthen my students' understanding of and connection to the writing process. I point to them often. After my students have internalized them, the quotes come down and new ones go up. I try to post a quote from an author whose work we've read. This one is an exception because most everyone knows *Charlie and the Chocolate Factory,* and in my reading workshop we soon start *Fantastic Mr. Fox* (on audiocassette, in Roald Dahl's voice). The World Wide Web is a wonderful resource. You can go to http://www.roalddahl.com and hear this quote and more in his own voice.

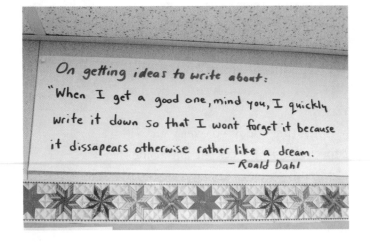

Mini-Lesson: Meaningful Objects

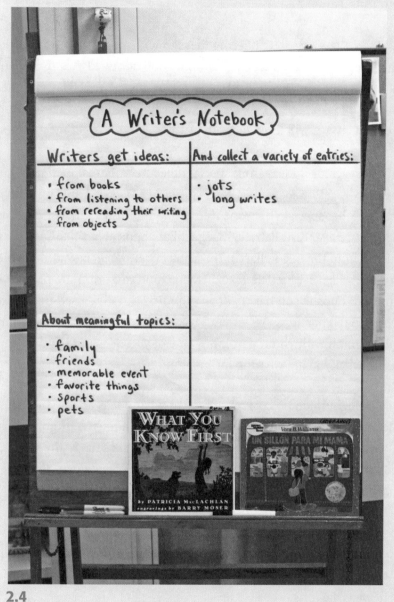

2.4

Teaching point: Writers get ideas of what to write about from objects. Before you begin, briefly review the pie chart, the coming-to-carpet procedure, and how you expect students to sit with their notebooks and, today, with their objects or photos as well. Then call them to the carpet with their objects, notebooks, and pencils and, as always, say, "Check yourselves," or the like, as a signal for total attention before starting your mini-lesson.

Connect: "Writers, we are gathering ideas to write about in our notebooks, ideas that are meaningful to us. You are getting good at quickly capturing your ideas on your jot pages, just like Roald Dahl does. [*Share quote.*] Yesterday, our ideas and memories were unlocked by a book we read and by thinking and talking and listening to each other. Today, we will look at another way that writers get meaningful ideas."

Teach: "Writers can get ideas from special objects or photos. I am going to add that to our growing list. Yesterday we read *A Chair for My Mother*. I am sure every time the author sits in that special chair, she thinks about the story that she told us in her book. Yesterday, we also read Patricia MacLachlan's book *What You Know First*. Now listen to this bit from the inside flap of the book cover. [*Read how the author carries a bag of prairie dirt with her.*] Patricia MacLachlan could not bring the prairie with her when she moved, but she still has that bag of prairie dirt. She used that object to remember and to tell her story. Yesterday, I asked each of you to bring an important object or photograph with you today. If any one of you does not have an object, then consider using what you are wearing for inspiration."

Model: "I brought this photo of myself taken when I was about your age. I am wearing a favorite dress, two of my three sisters are standing next to me, I can see my neighborhood in the background, and I am reminded of so, so many stories I need to jot them down so I won't forget them." [*Model being quiet and thoughtful with your object or photo and jotting ideas on your jot page.*]

Practice: "Now it's your turn. You will do a "think, talk, and write." First think about what you'd like to say about your object, then talk to your neighbor, then write your jots. After you have both shared and made jots, we will talk and share out to the group before we write long."

2.5 | The Turn-and-Talk Share

Talking before writing builds your community and helps students find, formulate, and fine-tune ideas. But we need to teach how to talk and listen to each other respectfully, by turning to face each other, using eye contact and wait time. Some boys do not appear to listen intently to each other. I have read that boys are uncomfortable with direct eye contact—or maybe it's just the second day of school. When I asked, however, each of these boys could talk about the other's drumstick or soccer trophy and its meaning to its owner. For some, the second day may not be a comfortable time for an intimate, knee-to-knee turn-and-talk. While I don't enforce eye contact, and there can be spaces between the pair, these boys and all students need to learn to be comfortable facing each other as a sign of respect and intent.

Link and Excuse to Write

Before excusing your students to write, be clear about next steps and expectations at closure. Tell them, "For our independent writing time, your first job is to choose one jot that is tugging at you and then your second job is to write long. Today, at closure, we will be sharing some of your writing, the meaningful memories that your objects or photos unlocked."

When I was 2 years old,

I was playing jumprope with my

(cosin) and my grandmother.

When I was playing jumprope

I fall down and _____ my forehead.

2.6 | Mid-Workshop Teach: Spelling

After you write for a few minutes and as you are walking around smiling and nodding, you may notice the need for a mid-workshop teach. Mid-workshop teaching points in these early days are quick global strategies to help your student writers keep their writing flowing—quick teaching points that don't need a whole mini-lesson and writing workshop hour to themselves. Mini-lessons need to stay focused, not cluttered with little add-on teaching points. You want to teach those little add-ons at an opportune time. Say, "Excuse me, writers. I see and hear that some of you are getting stuck with spelling. As writers, you have some choices. You can look up the word in your "Quick-Word" if you think you can hang on to your thought or circle the word and keep going so you don't lose your thought, then come back to your circled words later. If you don't know or can't remember the word you want to use, draw a line and fill in the blank later; if you know the word or phrase in your first language, but not in English, then write in your first language and translate later. The point is, don't let any one word interrupt your flow of thinking and your writing. Choose a strategy that works for you and your situation and keep going."

(continued)

To excuse I always say, "If you know what to do, look at me, and I'll excuse you." This is a check for me that everyone understands and will be applying the mini-lesson to his or her own plan of action for the day. If anyone is left on the carpet, looking down while I excuse everyone else, then I can manage that student's issues right then. When I occasionally have half the class or more looking down, then I know my lesson bombed. If the same student(s) stay every day just for extra attention, call them on it. If a student looks at you to be excused but doesn't get to work, and/or later says he doesn't know what to do, call him on it. After everyone is excused, I stand at the front of the room, quietly, just looking to see how they are doing getting started. That seems to help them settle down. After students have gotten to work, spend a few minutes writing off your photo or object so you can relate to your students in conferring and in closure. It is very powerful to model the act of writing and show what that concentrated effort looks like.

Conferring

Someday soon, you will feel that walking around and smiling and nodding and saying little bits of encouragement aren't enough. Then you'll know you are ready to start developing the heart of your workshop—conferences with individual students. I refer you to Carl Anderson's book *How's It Going?* for all you need to become skilled at conferring (well, his book and lots and lots of practice). I also refer you to Nancie Atwell's *In the Middle* (1998, pp. 226–229), where you'll find a list of "questions that can help." This is the list I used when I first started conferring. I have also provided you with a master in Appendix C that you can keep on your clipboard until you get the conference structure internalized. For most of your conferring this week, it's all about your students learning to generate writing that has meaning for them. It's not about correcting and editing student writing. It's about helping your writers become independent. Be careful with your wording. Say, "What are you working on?" not, "How can I help you?" Have a conversational tone—writer to writer. Compliment the student on something well done. "You got started right away" or "I can see you are thinking thoughtfully about ideas." Mostly just listen with great interest as they tell their stories to you. Ask questions to help them get at more detail. Then say something global that they can use now and in the future, something like, "I'd like to teach you a writer's strategy. When writers have a blank page in front of them, one way to find the words to write is to say them out loud and then write down what you heard yourself say. You can talk to a classmate or to yourself. Today, you've just talked to me. Do you remember what you said? Great! Then what should you do? Excellent! You've just learned a writer's strategy that you can use anytime."

2.7 | Closure: Sharing Meaningful Writing

Call your students back to the carpet with about 15 minutes left in the hour. Plan for about ten minutes for sharing memories and five minutes for using the chart as shown below in photo 2.8. Today at closure, you are continuing to help your students understand why people write, that writing has meaning. Have them warm up by sharing with each other why what they wrote about has meaning for them before they share out to the group.

Note: In writing, it is sometimes difficult for writers to put their finger on why what they have written has meaning to them. We are teachers, a patient lot. We can remember that writing is often a journey of discovery. We know how to celebrate our students' efforts, however wobbly and uncertain. We know how to guide and prod them to deeper thinking and clearer articulation and how that looks and sounds at all their different ages and developmentally appropriate levels. I remind you to keep your expectations high.

2.8 | Starting the Writing Habits Chart

Notice, label, and chart the good writing habits that your students are developing. We nurture and grow what we focus on.

Writing Habits	
What Good Writers Do	**Why** Writers Do That
• capture ideas in notebook	• so ideas aren't lost, forgotten
• reread	• to remember more and to keep going
• reread	• to trigger new meaningful ideas
• write about meaningful topics	• to better understand ourselves & to share and to connect w/other people

Management Note

How did your independent writing time go today? After you wrote and walked around, were you able to confer with at least a few students and give your total attention to your conferees? Your modeling and all the talking and sharing should be generating more than enough enthusiasm for a roomful of students to sustain their writing during the independent writing time. It should. But perhaps it didn't. Do you need to lengthen the students' talking time and shorten the writing time, especially for younger students? You can gradually build up to a longer writing period. Many students still need to talk about their ideas and their writing during the independent writing time, so make sure you're allowing for that. Is the talk you're hearing at a low voice level and on task? Do you and your students need to co-construct a "Looks Like, Sounds Like" chart?

2.9 | Homework Try-It

Let your students know that tomorrow they will be sharing their writing from the night before with their neighbor, and that you expect a meaningful entry. Remind them that the Try-It is a suggestion. Be sure to chant and pantomime "write, write, write, backpack."

Try-it:
Choose a jot
and write long

Digging Deeper
for Meaning

Overview

You are continuing to build your rituals and routines. You are continuing to emphasize that writers write about memories, ideas, and information that they find meaningful. That is why writing is interesting to do and interesting to read.

Note for younger grades: You may want to save today's "Digging Deeper" lesson for the third week of the launch, after students have chosen a seed idea. Or teach this lesson today and repeat it again in Week 3.

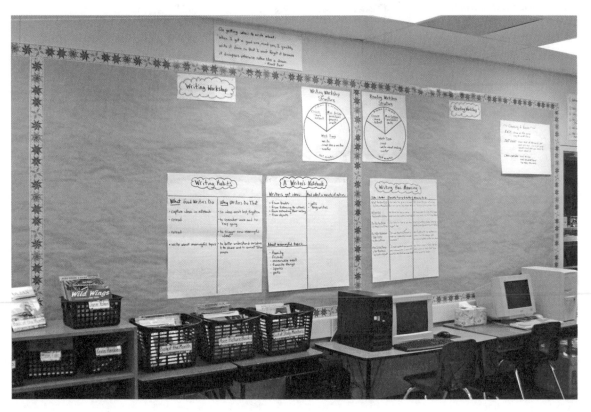

3.1 | Chart Walls

My walls look like this after the second day and before starting the third.

3.2 | Books to Enjoy Today as First Reads

To set up tomorrow's mini-lesson, read two books that differ greatly in terms of intended audience and genre. I like to use Jane Yolen's *How Do Dinosaurs Say Goodnight?* (or any of this series) and *Welcome to the Green House*. As always, be sure to model and leave time for jotting as well as time to add to your

Writing Has Meaning chart, asking why Jane Yolen wrote these books, and emphasizing that the same author can write many different kinds of literature. You'll find Yolen's explanation for how and why she started the *Dinosaurs* series on her Web site.

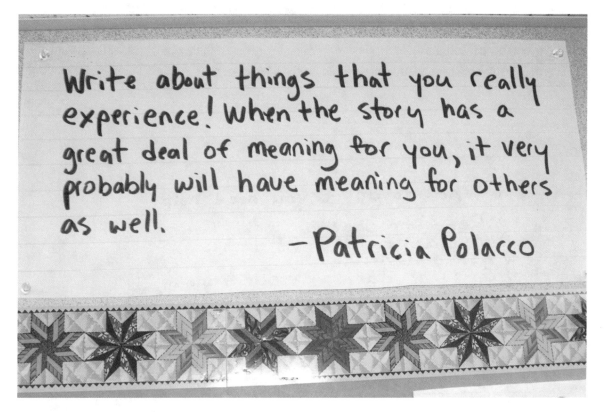

Write about things that you really experience! When the story has a great deal of meaning for you, it very probably will have meaning for others as well.

—Patricia Polacco

3.3 | Author Support

Have this quote up, as it supports today's mini-lesson and your ongoing work.

3.4 | Before the Call to Carpet: Getting Help Chart

This is a permanent chart, reduced to its smallest possible size. I place it up high, near my author quotes. You could choose to take the time to teach this chart in a procedural mini-lesson as part of your workshop. But in this first week, I prefer to teach more writing strategies in my mini-lessons and to review this chart ahead of the workshop. When you talk about getting help from mentor texts, explain, "The word *mentor* means teacher. So far, we've been using books to get ideas to write about and to understand that writing has meaning. We'll use books and other texts as mentors all year in different ways to help us learn more about writing." The red and green tags serve as a quick visual cue for me as I survey the room during independent writing time. Red tags mean "Please don't bother me or I will lose my train of thought." The green tag means the student has exhausted all other resources and would like a teacher conference. When you sit down to confer with a student who set out a green tag, first ask what he or she tried before deciding to ask for help. You have the right, of course, to veto red and green tags. From now on, if a student comes to you asking for help, give a nonverbal response with no eye contact. Simply point to the chart. Otherwise you risk enabling teacher-dependent behaviors. On this day of introduction to this premade chart, hold up your clipboard and conference top sheet showing all the students' names in boxes, and make a big point of showing how there is only one of you and many of them. Getting help from the teacher should be their last resort.

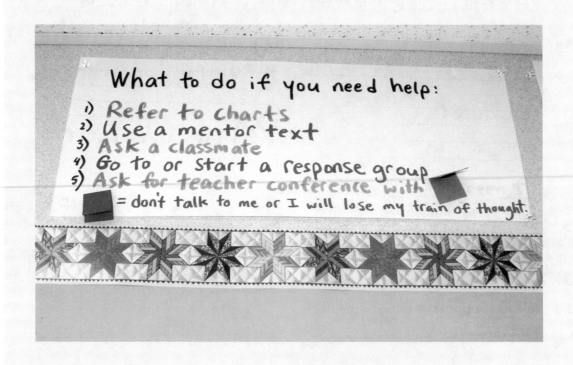

3.5 | Mini-Lesson: Digging Deeper, a Personal Journey

Teaching point: Writers think deeply to find the meaning of their writing.

Mini-Lesson: Digging Deeper, a Personal Journey

Call to the carpet with notebooks and pencils: "Check yourselves."

Connect: "Writers, we have spent the last two days gathering ideas to write about in our notebooks. We've been jotting our ideas and writing long about the ones that were tugging at us. Today, instead of gathering more new ideas, let's look more deeply, more closely, at one piece of writing that we have already."

Teach: "It takes time and thought for writers to develop their ideas. All that time and thought is well worth it to the writer and to the reader. Yesterday we read *When I Was Young in the Mountains*. Cynthia Rylant knows how important it is to know why you are writing and that it is also important to tell your reader. [*Reread last page of Rylant's book.*] Like all good writers, Patricia Polacco also knows the importance of meaning in writing and she has said so. [*Point to author quote.*] When Patricia started to work on *My Rotten Redheaded Older Brother*, she knew it was meaningful to her, because it is about her family, but she probably didn't discover why her story had so much meaning until she really thought long and hard about it."

Model: "Writers, I am going to model now what I'd like you to do. First I am going to reread my long-writes and listen for my heart to tell me which one I want to think more deeply about. [*Model rereading.*] It's this one here, this one about when I tried out for the school choir when I was in second grade. [*Reread silently, nodding and thinking.*] I want to say more about what I am thinking, I want to say what comes from my heart, and I want to share with my reader why this piece is important to me. To help me figure that out, I am going to use a web. I am going to draw what I am thinking on this chart paper, so we can look at it together. Some of you may not want to do a web like this—you may have a different way to get at deeper meaning. Whatever works for you is fine."

Practice: "Now it's your turn to take some quiet time here with your writing and reread, choosing one entry and thinking about what you are really trying to say. On the blank page opposite the entry you are thinking deeper about, draw your thinking in a way that works for you. I'll give you some time here, and then we'll have a turn-and-talk, followed by a whole-group share to help us develop our ideas further. If you finish your thinking and you need to write, do so while you are waiting."

Link and excuse to write: "In your independent writing time today, follow this new, deeper direction and understanding that you have and add more to the entry you are focusing on. Or, if you need to, keep digging. At closure today, you will be sharing why the writing you are working on is important to you and what you wrote to share that importance with your reader. If you know what to do, look at me, and I'll excuse you."

Note about your own writing: What is your best choice for your class? Do they need to see you writing for a few minutes with them? At this point in my launch, I have written a little the night before so I will be able to relate to my students in conferring and in closure. I want to share how I first thought I knew the meaning of my piece, but when I thought more deeply, I discovered a new meaning, what I really was trying to say. I am anxious to spend more time conferring in class now, to help more of them dig deeper.

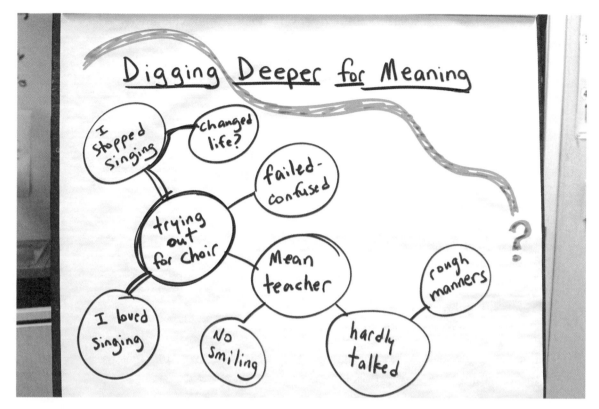

3.6 | Mid-Workshop Teach

Sometimes you won't see the need for a mid-workshop teach. Sometimes you'll see the need to reinforce your mini-lesson by sharing a student's success to help others who are grappling. Sometimes you will see the need to reteach your point in a different way. This abstract lesson is very difficult for many third and fourth graders. I stopped the writing time mid-way and used a path metaphor: "Class, I see many of you are struggling. I'd like to try a different way of explaining what I mean by digging for deeper meaning. When you are walking in a new place, down a new street, or down a forest path, you don't know what will be around the corner or around the bend. Yet you keep going because you are curious and you want to know. Finding deeper meaning is a journey. It may not come quickly, but if you stick with it and keep going, keep thinking, and continue your web, it will come."

Conferring

Sometimes, the writer's strategy you teach in your mini-lesson won't work for some of your writers. That's where conferring can be so helpful in meeting a specific student's needs.

I had a conference with my youngest third grader, a boy reading below grade level. He was writing about a trip to a lake with his family. He said he didn't know why it was so meaningful. He wanted to try to discover his deeper meaning but the web wasn't working for him. I told him that another strategy for discovering deeper meaning is to ask yourself questions or find someone who will help you by asking questions. I said I'd do that for him. It went something like this:

TEACHER: How far down the path of discovery do you think you are?

STUDENT: Maybe halfway.

TEACHER: Was this about being with your family that day, is that it?

STUDENT: Nope.

TEACHER: Is this a first-time story about a boat ride?

STUDENT: Yes, but that's not quite it. I jumped off the boat into deep water. [*He hadn't written that part yet.*]

TEACHER: Is that it?

STUDENT: Yeah, I was brave.

TEACHER: Did you know that about yourself, that you are a brave person?

STUDENT: No. I never knew that before.

TEACHER: Wow, then that was a really big day for you—no wonder you chose this day to write about. Are you going to tell your reader why this piece is so meaningful to you, like Patricia Polacco does in *Thunder Cake*?

STUDENT: Yeah.

TEACHER: Where are you going to add that?

STUDENT: I think at the end here.

3.7 | Reminder: Keeping Track of Conferences

Keep track of who you have been conferring with. This sheet is a quick check for me. I need to be sure I am not spending more time with students I think need more help, thus enabling them to be dependent on me. And I never want to abandon my gifted kids. Children need to feel they are capable of functioning on their own and deserve an equal opportunity to be pushed to their own fullest potential.

3.8 | Closure: Sharing Writing

Have a Turn-and-Talk share, then a whole-class share about the process. Reinforce your teaching point: It takes extra thought and time to get at the meaning of one's writing. It's a journey of discovery and sometimes a surprise to the writer. Share and label all the good work your writers have done.

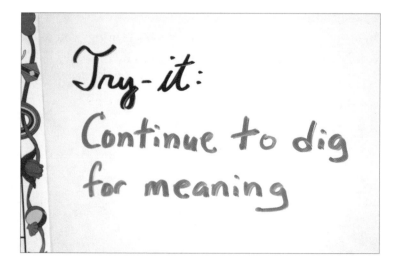

3.9 | Writing Habits Chart

Here I elaborated the third bullet, adding *think deeply* to the second reread. Add to your Writing Habits chart in a way that makes sense for you and your students, making your additions authentic and relevant to the work of the day.

3.10 | Homework Try-It

Digging for meaning is important work that takes time. Talk with your students about how the mind will "back-burner" ideas, and let them know that when they are writing tonight in their notebooks, they may make a new discovery or further develop one from today.

The Heart Map

Overview

A well-run writing workshop is a very fluid place. You not only have to understand the goals of your unit but also continually assess where your student writers are, what their needs are, and what your next best steps should be to reach your main goals and as many students as possible. There should never be a different item every day from a buffet of writers' strategies. Your lessons should always follow a thread of thought and logic, allowing your students to construct deeper understandings over time. Your conferring, both with individuals and with small groups of students with similar needs, is where the individual instruction will powerfully advance your writers, from their unique places of meaning construction.

On this day, based on your class, your grade level, how far your students got yesterday, and what your lesson was, you may decide to repeat or review yesterday's lesson and give them more time to pursue that one piece of writing that may have taken a different turn and needs more time.

After yesterday's deep dig, reinforced with the reading work and the Writing Has Meaning chart, students are beginning to understand that good writing comes from a very individual place, a writer's heart. So today I prefer to give my students time to take a step back and have more time to be introspective. And on this fourth day, our community is feeling safer to most students, a requirement for this lesson that asks students to share so much of themselves.

Note for younger grades: You likely took two days for Day 1, then one day for writing off an object, and skipped the deep dig, which brings you to today—a great day for your young writers to further access meaningful ideas by drawing.

Regarding routines and rituals—Congratulations! You have covered the basics. Review throughout the year as needed.

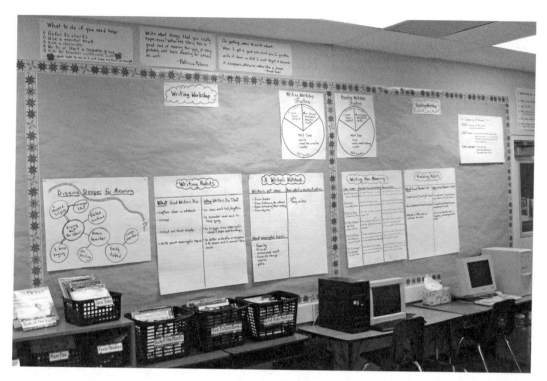

4.1 | Chart Walls

My chart walls look like this after Day 3 and before Day 4.

4.2 | Books to Enjoy Today as First Reads

I don't want to read only narratives, because then my students may write only narratives, and a writer's notebook should be filed with all sorts of different writing. I want my students to know they have a choice of structure as well as topic. That thinking is behind the book choices from yesterday and today. One writer writes in different genres and for different audiences. Yolen's *Wild Wings* and *Least Things* are wonderful because both are two genres in one— poetry and informational text on every page. As always, be sure to model and leave time for jotting. And add to your Writing Has Meaning chart. In this case, Jane Yolen tells you all about how she came to write *Least Things*. You'll find it on her Web site, http://www.janeyolen. com. Click on *Works*, then *Poetry*, and then on the picture of the book.

Jane Yolen's **Advice** for **Young** **Writers:**
#1 Read, read, read!
#2 Write, write, write!

g Workshop
tructure

Reading W
Struc

Drawing helps a writer find meaningful topics to write about.

4.3 | Author Support

Making strong connections between reading and writing work is powerful instruction. You've started this already with the Writing Has Meaning chart and posting and referring to author quotes. About now I add a very informal author study that connects and supports the work in my reading workshop and my writing workshop. I like to study Jane Yolen because her body of work is huge and varied. She writes in so many genres and across so many reading levels. Students need to know that they, like all writers, have choices with respect to genre and audience. Her Web site is a great resource. You can look things up or assign students to do the research and share what she has to say about her reading and writing life, habits, and processes, as well as her books. She has a video about her reading and writing life and processes, which I found for sale, used. She has also written a book for writers, *Take Joy*, which I have learned so much from and love to quote from to my students.

Conferring

As you are standing at the front of the room, watching students settle into this activity and deciding who to confer with, remember that this is a wonderful opportunity to get to know your students better, to make a special connection with a challenging student or with those who are especially reticent or shy.

4.4 | Mini-Lesson: Heart Map

Teaching points: Writers draw and sketch to find meaningful ideas to write about. Writers write from the heart and in many different genres. This heart map idea is straight from Georgia Heard's book *Awakening the Heart*, a must-have for your writing workshop poetry unit.

Before the lesson, I draw the outline of a heart on 8.5 x 11 paper and photocopy a stack for students who would like to use a starter heart shape. I use standard-sized paper because students will tape these into their notebooks, as a place to go for topic ideas in any genre.

Mini-Lesson: Heart Map

Call to the carpet empty-handed: "Check yourselves."

Connect: "Writers, we did some deep thinking yesterday, digging into the meaning of what we write so we can express that meaning for ourselves and our readers. That's what writers do. Today we will continue to think about what is meaningful to us, what is in our hearts."

Teach: "Writers write about and share what is important to them, what they care about. One strategy for thinking about what is important to you is to draw yourself a heart map."

Explain: "I got this heart map idea from a wonderful poet named Georgia Heard, who wrote this book for teachers about teaching children to write poetry. It such a helpful book—I use it every year. This is my own nearly finished heart map. When I look at my heart map, I get all sorts of ideas for writing projects that I would like to work on. We know Jane Yolen writes about many different things in many different kinds of writing, many different genres. When I look at just this one little piece of my heart map, this drawing here of my flower garden, I think I could write a poem about flowers, or an informational piece about snails, or a how-to about planting carpet roses, or a narrative that tells the story of how I broke a water pipe with my shovel when I was digging a big hole to plant a new tree. All of my little drawings give me many ideas. The point is, everything here is very, very important to me. Every writer's heart map will look different because we are each unique individuals. I also have here a heart map that a former student made and let me borrow to show you. See how his is different from mine. See, too, how it is bigger. I used to have students make them big like this, but then we learned they wouldn't fit in our writer's notebooks where we need them to get ideas. It's another resource, along with your jot page."

Practice: "First, take some time and think quietly about what you will have on your heart map. Is there is one very important thing that you want to put in the middle? [*Make some age-appropriate comment here to your class that alleviates any anxiety about the quality of the drawings.*] Next, decide if you will take a plain piece of paper from the back table when I excuse you and draw your own heart outline, or will you take the paper with the photocopied heart outline."

(continued)

Link and excuse to write: "At closure, we'll take some time to share our drawings and what is meaningful in our lives. Some of you may finish before closure; if you do, write jots and/or an entry off your heart map, or you can continue working on what you were writing yesterday. If you know what to do, look at me, and I'll excuse you."

4.5 | Closure: Sharing Writing

Plan for lots of time here, 10 to 15 minutes at least. Reinforce your teaching point. This is a strategy; making a drawing can help writers find heartfelt topics to write about. Allow for lots of talking and sharing; it's invaluable time spent that will strengthen your community and set your writers up for success in their future writing projects.

Writing Habits

What Good Writers Do	Why Writers Do That
• Capture ideas in notebook	• So ideas aren't lost, forgotten
• reread	• to remember more and to keep going
• reread and think deeply	• to trigger new meaningful ideas & deeper understandings
• write about meaningful topics	• to better understand ourselves & to share and to connect with other people
• draw, sketch	• to find meaningful topics

A Writer's Notebook

Writers get ideas:	And collect a variety of entries:
• from books • from listening to others • from rereading their writing • from objects • from drawing a ♡ map	• jots • long writes • memories • poems • lists • information • sketches and drawings

About meaningful topics:

- family
- friends
- memorable event
- favorite things
- sports
- pets

4.6 | Writing Habits and Writer's Notebook Charts

Keep adding to these charts. Make your additions authentic and relative to the work you've done so far in your classroom.

4.7 | Homework Try-It

Before excusing your students to go home today, and before the "write, write, write, backpack" chant, this fourth day is a good time to reinforce why they should be writing at home. Remind them the more we write, the better we get. You can also check to see that they understand that the Try-It is a suggestion and ask, if they are not doing a Try-It, what other kinds of meaningful entries they are doing as thoughtful writers: dreams, hopes, poems, lists, whatever. Be sure to honor their choices and ideas by adding them to your Writer's Notebook chart.

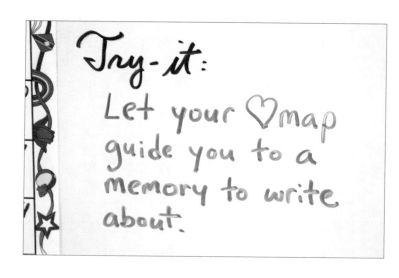

Try-it: Let your ♡map guide you to a memory to write about.

Wiggle-Room Day

Overview

To decide what to do today, check the goals of the week and assess your progress. Consider these possibilities:

- You've already used this day because you determined your class needed two days on another day's lesson.

- You need a second day to complete the heart map work.

- The week's goals have been reached, and it's appropriate to move on to Week 2. Go for it.

- You have a fast, older class and you want students to learn more ways to generate ideas. Some suggestions:

    1. Drawings are a great way to dig up vivid memories. Students could draw a neighborhood map, a map of the inside of their home, or the map of a specific place.
    2. Free-writes are a stream-of-consciousness form of writing. No punctuation, no picking up the pencil, just five minutes or more of brain-dumping to see what's locked up in there, followed by a reread to pick up a meaningful thread of an idea for writing long.

5.1 | Books to Enjoy Today as First Reads

Be sure to read *Hello Ocean: Hola Mar* by Pam Muñoz Ryan sometime today or Monday morning before you start your Day 6 mini-lesson. It's a descriptive piece that includes all the senses and lots of wonderful sense-specific vocabulary. It will serve to teach or to review the five senses to prepare for next week. You can also go to http://www.scholastic.com and show the video interview with Pam Muñoz Ryan where she talks about her writing process.

Also, read *Owl Moon* and maybe one other book to set up the Day 6 lesson about the sensory detail of sound in writing. *What You Know First* is another good choice for sound, and you've already read it. It is also time to start directing the discussions after these first read-alouds into a new direction—the purpose behind the detail. To preload for Day 6, after your read-aloud, ask why Jane Yolen included the sound of trains and dogs at the start of *Owl Moon*. How does sound help draw the reader in and make that setting real?

Week 2

Writing With Sensory Details

Four Goals

- Continue building a safe and productive writing community

- Develop the understanding—revision is a regular and ongoing part of the writing process

- Develop the understanding—good writing has purposeful detail

- Generate lots of thinking, talk, and writing

Overview of Week 2

The focus of this second week is on detail in writing, specifically sensory detail. This is the beginning of the work you will be doing all year in different genre and craft studies. It's the beginning of showing your students how to look closely and notice how writing is crafted to convey the author's meaning. You want your students to understand that it is the *purposeful* placement of detail in their writing that develops and delivers the meaning of the piece to the reader while making the writing very real for the reader. Be sure to include other genres besides narrative as your mentors because your launch is meant to help students understand what *all* good writing has. As you explore writing with a focus on the purposeful use of sensory detail this week, be sure to reinforce the ideas about meaning from last week so they are not forgotten.

It is best not to compress this week; studying one sense per day will allow your students to construct deeper meaning. You want your students to develop a solid foundation of understanding about the use of sensory detail in writing and to layer in other understandings, such as:

- Revision is a regular and ongoing part of the writing process, something separate from editing and not saved for one "revision day."

- Writers make thoughtful, purposeful choices.

- The writer's term "craft" is both a noun and a verb and has broad meaning.

You can do the senses in any order, of course. But over the years, I have found an order that I think works best. The sense of hearing is first, because it's easy to isolate. Touch, also easy to isolate, is next, but separating how something feels to the touch, as opposed to how a person feels, may be a challenge to convey. I introduce sight next, the sensory detail most heavily used in writing. The practice of isolating the first two helps students isolate sight. Last we explore the sensory detail of smell; by this day students are curious and ready to search for this less frequently used sensory detail in our mentor texts. Taste is so rarely used outside of the cookbook genre that I will usually just mention how rare it is and fold it into our "smell day" if we happen to find any examples.

Each day is structured very similarly, focusing on one sense per day, giving your students a lot of predictable practice developing observation skills, purposeful revision skills, and building their vocabulary. You have just two charts to start and add to this week: Writing With Sensory Detail and Vocabulary for Sensory Detail. In addition, you'll need to add a little to your Writing Habits and A Writer's Notebook charts that you started last week.

Adjusting the Week for Yourself, Your Class, and Grade Level

You now know how fast your students learn and what their needs are, and you can plan your workshop hour accordingly. Be sure to allow enough time for revision work in existing notebook entries where students will add the sensory detail of the day to their writing. This is a wonderful and fun week for the students, with lots of observation time. If you didn't turn around any grumpy-about-writing attitudes last week, with your focus on meaning, this week should hook those hold-backs. Remember, while this sensory detail focus is highly engaging, it will all be for naught without the critical last step—applying this learning every day to their own writing. The lessons also layer in a focus on purpose that gradually grows more complicated in understanding and application each day. Adjust the concept of purposeful details up or down to a developmentally appropriate level of thought and application for your grade.

Suggestions for Supporting Work to Do in Your Reading Workshop

See Day 10 for a necessary reading lesson to do sometime before Week 3. You might use these ideas now, or later, or revisit them in future units of study:

- At reading workshop closure, students share an example of the sense of the day that they found in their independent reading and discuss the author's purpose.

- Possible inquiry questions for individuals or small groups in your informal author study: Does Jane Yolen use sensory detail in all her writing across all genres? Where does she use which sensory details, and for what purpose?

- This is an excellent week to begin work in visualization and schema connections that readers use for reading comprehension, because to visualize and connect, a reader uses those sensory details that the writer purposefully provides.

- You are using picture books as mentors in your writing workshop mini-lessons, but you will notice that the chapter books you are using for whole-class read-alouds will have the same writers' craft. Point this out when the opportunity arises. For instance, when I read *Junie B. Jones* books by Barbara Park at the beginning of the year, we laugh and enjoy them; subsequently, anyone at that reading level is comfortable being seen with a *Junie B. Jones* book for his or her independent reading. As we explore sensory details in writing this week, on Day 6, I can refer to *Junie B. Jones and the Stupid Smelly Bus*, for instance, with the janitor's "jingly keys." On Day 9, I can remind students how Junie B. sniffed the Band-Aids that "smell just like a brand-new beach ball."

Supporting Work for Your Language Use and Conventions Block

- You'll be starting and adding to a sensory detail vocabulary chart over the course of this week and into the school year as students continue to discover more vocabulary.

- Add to your spelling strategies and punctuation work when appropriate.

- Continue to have students self-edit their writing homework every morning.

Supporting Daily Homework and Homework Share

This week change your Try-It to a Do-It because you will want to keep the extended writing practice at home focused on developing sensory observation and word choice skills. Decide if you need to continue the "write, write, write, backpack" chant and pantomime at the end of the day.

Continue the notebook check and share first thing in the morning. Share struggles and successes. Students should then do a quick self-edit for whatever conventions they should know so far. Continue your informal assessment by checking to see if they are understanding the lesson of the day to the point where the concept is apparent in the writing that they do on their own at home.

I do ask about and encourage writing over the weekend. After all, a real writer's notebook is with the writer at all times. Students who used their notebooks will share, and we applaud their writer's life. But I do not officially check notebooks on Mondays.

Note: If you are seeing parental involvement in a child's writing homework, consider sending home a letter explaining what a writer's notebook is, that the student will not be graded on the content, and how important it is that no one besides the student writer, not even the teacher, makes marks or corrections in the notebook. I find it helps to show my messy notebook to parents at Back to School Night and at parent-teacher conferences as well, if necessary.

Exploring Sensory Details—
Sound

Overview

We'll start with the sense of hearing. You enjoyed Jane Yolen's free-verse narrative poem *Owl Moon* and Cynthia Rylant's descriptive piece *Night in the Country* last week as first reads with your students. Both are wonderful examples of writers using the sensory detail of sound to help bring the writing to life for the reader. Upper grades could also refer back to *What You Know First*. Your focus today will also continue to develop your students' writing identities by connecting Yolen's and Rylant's work to their own writing.

Keep in mind that it's Monday. My students always benefit from reviews on Mondays. In addition, establish your expectations for behavior by taking your class outside and/or around the school to practice their sensory observations this week.

6.1 | Chart Walls

Here is my entire literacy wall—Reading Workshop, Writing Workshop, and Language Use and Conventions—after Week 1 and before Week 2.

6.2 | Books to Enjoy Today as First Reads

To prepare for tomorrow, you'll need a book like *My Father's Hands* which has obvious examples of the sensory detail of touch. *Owl Moon* is also a very good choice, and you've already read it.

As always, leave time for jotting, for you and your students. Then consider whether to add to your Writing Has Meaning chart. Is just an open discussion appropriate? What do your students need to continue to deepen their understanding of writing for meaning? Consider your grade level and grade-level standards. Are you building these types of discussions into a foundation for present or future literary essays? Or will a simple understanding that the author likes bugs, or likes being with her dad, suffice?

Today, I begin to direct the thinking in our read-alouds and in reading workshop to noticing how the writer provides the reader with details to help the reader visualize and make connections to the story.

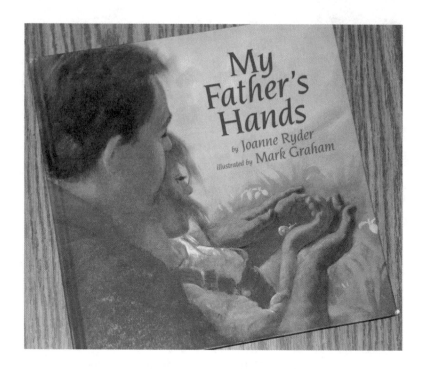

Readers have expectations.
Writers have responsibilities.

6.3 | Author Support

This one is mine. It's a synthesis of all I have read and come to understand about the reading and writing connection. I leave this up all year and refer to it often because it sums up our work.

6.4 | Mini-Lesson: Exploring Sensory Details—Sound

Teaching point: Writers use sensory detail to draw in the reader; focus on sound.

You'll have two charts that you'll be using with each lesson this week: this one on sound and a vocabulary chart that you will start in closure. Your chart should look something like this at the start of your lesson.

A mini-lesson is called "mini" because it is supposed to be focused and short, less than ten minutes altogether, so there is plenty of writing time and share time every day. Last week, you controlled the length of your mini-lessons by sticking to one teaching point and doing most of the talking. This week you want to hear and record your students' ideas about purpose in the use of sensory details. You can stay under ten minutes if you and your class stay focused. Older students can decide which examples of sound to use, one from each book, and you can write the examples during the lesson. For younger children, choose your examples before the lesson and write them in before you start. There are no right answers to the question of purpose, only answers that make sense, so be careful not to play "guess what the teacher is thinking." Honor and write down what your students are thinking.

I like to use *Owl Moon* as my primary mentor text for this lesson. Of course, you may use any well-written bit of writing that focuses on sound from something you've already read. Have another familiar text, not narrative, that you can quickly show as a second example, such as the descriptive piece *Night in the Country* by Cynthia Rylant. Poetry or expository writing will also work; use any text already familiar to your students where writers have included sound.

Mini-Lesson: Exploring Sensory Details—Sound

Connect: "Writers, last week we did a lot of writing and reading and deep thinking. We learned that writing has meaning for the reader and the writer because that is what writing is—meaningful communication. [*Point to Writing Has Meaning chart.*] Readers expect to find meaning in what they read, and writers have a responsibility to their reader to craft meaningful writing. I have written these facts in two simple sentences: *Readers have expectations. Writers have responsibilities.* [*Point to this permanent chart.*] These two little sentences will guide our learning all year. Meaning, we've learned, is one expectation and responsibility of all readers. This week we will turn our attention to another expectation and responsibility—detail. We've started paying more attention to detail in writing as readers. As readers we can use the details a writer provides to visualize—to make pictures in our heads—so we can better understand what we are reading."

Teach: "Good writers know readers will be visualizing, so they pay close attention to adding detail to their writing. When writers use details that help a reader not only see, but also hear, touch, smell, and taste, like Pam Muñoz Ryan does in *Hello Ocean: Hola Mar*, that is called using sensory detail. Writers use sensory detail to make their writing come alive for their readers. This use of sensory detail is so important to good writing that we will spend all week studying it as readers and practicing using sensory detail as writers. Let's begin with the sensory detail of sound."

Explore: "I am going to read this part of *Owl Moon* where Jane Yolen writes to include the train and the dogs and feet crunching on the snow as Pa and his daughter set out. Then we will choose one bit of writing using sound from *Owl Moon* and think about *why* Jane Yolen put in the sound where she did. [*Record example and ideas about purpose.*] Yes, Jane Yolen made the setting real for us, and she created a mood with her word choices. I was thinking more about her writing, and I was imagining that she probably hears many train whistles and answering dogs from her farm in Michigan. She did what good writers do: she noticed the interesting sounds *and* she put them into words *and* she wrote those words down in her writer's notebook so her thoughts and word choices wouldn't just float away. When you notice the world around you *and* you find the words *and* you write down what you noticed, you are living the life of a writer. When it came time to write the setting for *Owl Moon*, those words were there for her, and she knew to use them because they are sounds that work well to make a farm setting at night real for her reader." [*If time permits, and if you think you need to, do a second example with* Night in the Country.]

Practice: "Let's practice this writing skill right now. Be very still and listen carefully . . . what do you hear?" [*It's amazing what you hear when you focus on listening in a silent room.*] Now let's find some words together to describe one thing that we've heard. [*Do this verbally.*] Now you try on your own. Stay on the carpet here, listen and think, choose words and write." [*Share out for a few minutes.*]

Link and excuse to write: "Our writing time will be in two parts today. First, we'll go outside to do more noticing and writing, because that's what writers do. Then, we'll do some very important work. You'll look back through your own writing, seeing where you can do a little revision work to add the sensory detail of sound. You'll have to think of where sound will work best in your writing, where it would be best to draw your reader in with sound. At closure you'll share what you added to your writing and why."

After the observation: When you are back inside, review and direct this revision piece by modeling looking through your own writing and finding a part where adding sound makes sense and will draw in your reader. Show how to use the skipped line to fit it in and how to use a caret, or how to use the opposite page with arrows.

6.5 | Sensory Detail Chart After the Mini-Lesson

Your chart might look like this *after* your mini-lesson, depending on examples chosen and what your students are thinking.

Writing with Sensory Detail		
Sense	Example	Purpose
Hearing	"They sang out, trains and dogs" OWL MOON	To make the setting real. To create a mood. Because next it gets really quiet.
	"Far over the hill you hear someone open and close a creaking screen door." NIGHT IN THE COUNTRY	To help you focus in and listen like you are there. To describe the night.

Conferring

Train yourself not to fix your students' writing. Continue to focus the conference on teaching writer's strategies such as thinking carefully about where to add sensory detail to writing. Have a mentor text with you, look at it together with your students, and talk about the author's choices, such as Jane Yolen's use of sensory detail in descriptions of the setting, and whether that would work in the student's piece.

6.6 | Closure: Word Choices and Revision Choices

You'll need a full ten minutes. You'll be managing two things at once: recording the vocabulary choices on a chart like this one and discussing your students' revision choices. Start by recording Yolen's word choices in *Owl Moon*, Rylant's choices in *Night in the Country*, and then add students' choices. This vocabulary chart will be used by your students as a scaffold and reference all year. I keep it on my Language Use and Conventions chart wall. You can continually add to it with words students find in their reading over the year.

In this closure, have students also share their thinking about purpose in their revision work. You could have a pair share first, then have a few students share out to the group. Or students could share their thinking about purposeful revision choices in small groups, then share revision and/or vocabulary choices with the whole group.

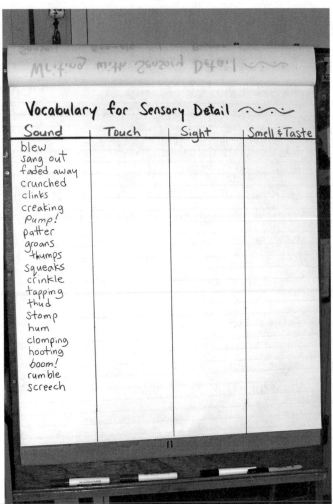

Writing Habits

What Good Writers Do	Why Writers Do That
• Capture ideas in notebook	• so ideas aren't lost, forgotten
• reread	• to remember more and to keep going
• reread and think deeply	• to trigger new meaningful ideas & deeper understandings
• write about meaningful topics	• to better understand ourselves & to share and to connect with other people
	• to find meaningful topics
• draw, sketch	
• use senses to observe & then write down what is noticed	• to improve writing skills, so writing will come alive for Reader
• revise their writing with thought and purpose	• to make it better

A Writer's Notebook

Writers get ideas:	And collect a variety of entries:
• from books • from listening to others • from rereading their writing • from objects • from drawing a ♡ map • from observing the world	• jots • long writes • memories • poems • lists • information • sketches and drawings • sensory observations • descriptions • conversations
About meaningful topics: • family • friends • memorable event • favorite things • sports • pets • nature	

6.7 | Writing Habits and Writer's Notebook Charts

Make authentic additions to these charts that are relevant to the work you are doing in your classroom.

6.8 | Homework Do-It

You'll need to turn your Try-It into a Do-It for this week to help your students internalize this work.

~~Try-it:~~ Do it:
Listen. Write what you hear.

Exploring Sensory Details—
Touch

Overview

Today you'll look at sensory details relating to touch. You will continue to layer in a lot of learning. Yesterday, you read aloud Joanne Ryder's *My Father's Hands* or another text or two that have examples of the sensory detail of touch to help bring the text to life for the reader. To prepare for today, go through *Owl Moon* and mark two places with sticky notes: one at the "icy hand was palm-down on my back" and another example that highlights the sense of touch. Also mark "prickly feet" and "soft and warm" in *My Father's Hands* with sticky notes so you can access these pages quickly.

7.1 | Chart Walls

After Day 6 and before Day 7, I rearrange my Language Use and Conventions chart wall to make room for the Vocabulary chart. I am using that repositionable glue because I'll be moving the Vocabulary chart and the Writing With Sensory Detail chart back and forth from wall to easel all week. Notice, too, I have started stacking charts. I have covered the Digging Deeper chart because we're focusing on sensory detail now.

It's still there, underneath, if someone needs to access the information. On my reading wall, I've moved two charts up to make room for my Reading Is Thinking chart. We've started work on visualizing and schemas in reading workshop to improve comprehension skills and to connect to our writing work in sensory details.

7.2 | Books to Enjoy Today as First Reads

Tomorrow, you can go back to *Owl Moon* for the sensory detail of sight. Yolen's descriptions are so wonderful, and you'll make the important point that writers use many senses in the same text. Or today read a favorite book of yours that paints vivid visual descriptions for the reader. Also, be sure to read a piece that has very few sight details for the reader, something fast-paced like "Gimmetheball" from *Rimshots* by Charles R. Smith, Jr. You'll need to be prepared to do a compare and contrast tomorrow between text that includes a lot of sensory sight detail and text that includes very little.

7.3 | Author Support

I use this quote to support our revision work this week. About this time I have started a chapter book, Roald Dahl's *Fantastic Mr. Fox* on audiotape, read by Dahl himself. All of my students have paperback copies, so they can follow along if they'd like to. We will discuss basic story elements and narrative structure for reading comprehension; this work begins to front-load the personal narrative writing unit of study that I have planned for after the launch. We also notice Dahl's carefully crafted writing, rich with sensory detail. I photographed this quote for you next to a book about Dahl written by his daughter. I highly recommend this book as a great resource for more quotes; for example, she writes that her father would revise one page of a story ten times. The book also has a two-page photograph of a draft of Dahl's in his longhand on yellow draft paper with circled revision work. When I show this to my students, who are doing the same kind of work on the same yellow draft paper, they feel very connected to a real writer.

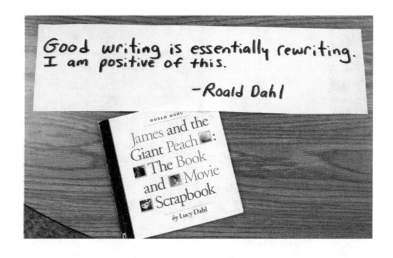

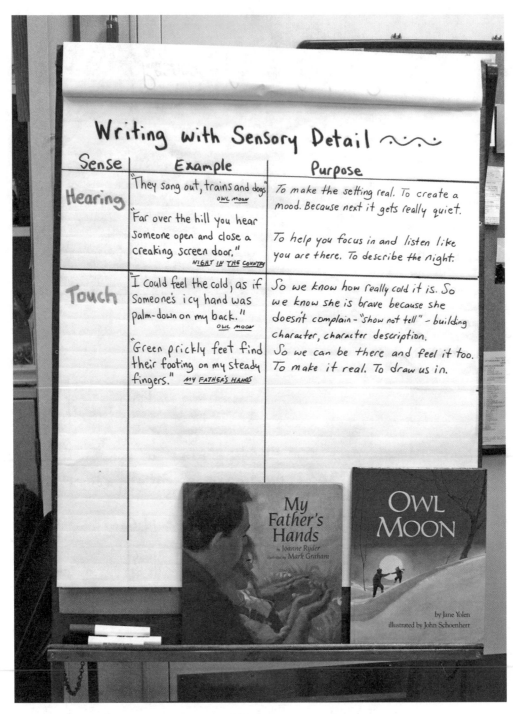

Writing with Sensory Detail ～・～

Sense	Example	Purpose
Hearing	"They sang out, trains and dogs" *OWL MOON*	To make the setting real. To create a mood. Because next it gets really quiet.
	"Far over the hill you hear someone open and close a creaking screen door." *NIGHT IN THE COUNTRY*	To help you focus in and listen like you are there. To describe the night.
Touch	"I could feel the cold, as if someone's icy hand was palm-down on my back." *OWL MOON*	So we know how really cold it is. So we know she is brave because she doesn't complain - "show not tell" - building character, character description.
	"Green prickly feet find their footing on my steady fingers." *MY FATHER'S HANDS*	So we can be there and feel it too. To make it real. To draw us in.

7.4 | Mini-Lesson: Exploring Sensory Details—Touch

Teaching point: Writers use sensory detail to draw the reader in; focus on touch. Your chart might be filled in like this after your mini-lesson and discussion, depending on the text you've used and your students' own ideas. Be ready to use *My Father's Hands* or your own choice, and also to go back to *Owl Moon* for examples of the sensory detail of touch. You might also look for examples in grade-level nonfiction texts.

Mini-Lesson: Exploring Sensory Details—Touch

Call to the carpet with notebooks and pencils: "Check yourselves."

Connect: "Writers, yesterday and for the rest of this week, we will be looking closely at sensory detail in writing. We are studying the choices writers make. Good writers craft their writing carefully. A writer's craft is everything a writer does to make the writing wonderful to read. One of the many, many choices writers make is whether to include the sensory detail of touch. That's our focus for today. Before we start, let's talk about the word *feel*. Feeling an emotion and feeling a breeze on your face are very different. Today we are talking about the latter." [*Discuss this until students grasp the distinction.*]

Teach: "We are learning that writers craft their writing with sensory detail to make it come alive for their readers. When you use the sensory detail of touch, you make your writing powerful because your readers can actually imagine feeling what you are describing. You can draw your reader in very close with this writers' strategy. Of course, as a writer, you want to be purposeful about where you draw your reader in."

Explore: "On this page in *Owl Moon*, Jane Yolen writes '. . . as if someone's icy hand was palm-down on my back.' Why is that an important detail to add? How does that detail help with the meaning of her story?" [*Discuss and record ideas.*]

"In *My Father's Hands* Joanne Ryder writes about the praying mantis's little feet on her hand. Why is that an important detail to add? How does that detail help with the meaning of her story? [*Discuss and record ideas.*] Please notice in these two books, neither writer uses the sensory detail of touch on every page. As you've noticed, writers are selective about where and how they develop details. Joanne Ryder does not describe how hard the porch feels when the girl sits on it, for instance. That's not an important detail in the story. What else does she choose not to describe? Why?"

Practice: "Just as with the sensory detail of sound, writers must carefully choose words to describe how something feels to the touch. Let's practice this skill right now. Jane Yolen wrote about the scarf and how it felt. Now you try that on your own. Choose something you are wearing, focus on how it feels, and then choose words to write about how it feels." [*Share out for a few minutes.*]

Link and excuse to write: "Just like yesterday, our writing time today will be in two parts. First, we'll go outside and focus just on our sense of touch. Then we'll come back in and do our thoughtful and purposeful revision work. At closure, we'll share and chart the vocabulary we used and share the choices we made in our revision work."

After the observation: When you are back in the classroom, model looking through your own writing and finding a place where you want to bring your reader in close. Review how to use the skipped line to fit the writing in, or use the opposite blank page.

Conferring

Continue to teach that writers think carefully about where to draw their reader in—and why. Use a mentor text in your conferring to support thinking and to teach that mentor texts are where student writers go for help.

7.5 | Closure: Sharing Writing

Record the vocabulary as it comes up. Discuss students' revision work and the process of choosing an important part of a notebook entry that would work for adding touch.

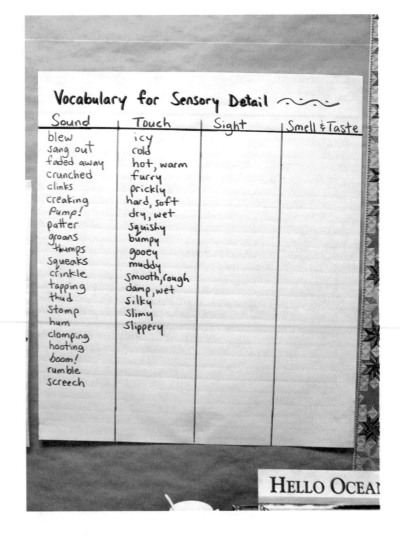

Writing Habits		Reading Habits	
What Good Writers Do	**Why Writers Do That**	**What Good Readers Do**	**Why Good Readers Do That**
• Capture ideas in notebook	• So ideas aren't lost, forgotten	• Choose (mostly) "Just Right" books	To understand & enjoy the book and learn a few new words
• reread	• to remember more and to keep going	• Use a bookmark to mark our place	So we don't lay the book flat open and damage the spine
• reread and think deeply	• to trigger new meaningful ideas & deeper understandings	• Reread a little when we continue the book	So we can remember what is happening, so the next part makes sense
• write about meaningful topics	• to better understand ourselves & to share and to connect with other people	• Think about & talk about books we've read	to help us understand the text, to hear what others think
• draw, sketch	• to find meaningful topics	• Notice writers' craft	to come back to it as writers to improve our own writing
• use senses to observe & then write down what is noticed	• to improve writing skills, so writing will come alive for Reader		
• revise their writing with thought and purpose	• to make it better		
• notice & study writers' craft	• to improve our own writing		

7.6 | Writing Habits Chart and Reading Habits Chart

I've put these side by side for this photo so you can see the similarity in the last line. During your launch, these charts will have grown according to your students' needs, your grade-level standards, and your goals. But the last line on both is an important connection to make and one you'll be revisiting all year long: noticing writer's craft to improve our own writing. These additions wrap up my writing and reading habits charts for now. I'll leave them up for a while longer as I continue to reinforce good habits by complimenting my students when I see good habits in use.

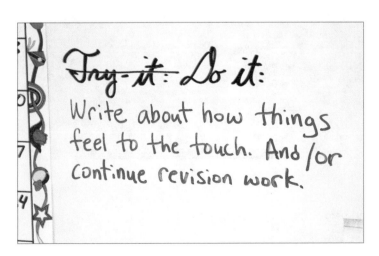

~~Try-it:~~ Do it:
Write about how things feel to the touch. And/or continue revision work.

7.7 | Homework Do-It

Again you'll need a Do-It. Your students need the extended practice to continue to construct meaning for themselves.

Exploring Sensory Details—
Sight

8.1 | Chart Walls

Here are my reading and writing walls, and part of my Language Use and
Conventions section after Day 7 and before Day 8.

Overview

Now that you've had separate discussions about hearing and touch, your students will find it easier to notice the sensory detail of sight as a separate sense. Today you will also be making a big point about purpose—that a writer stops the action or slows the story to describe how something looks in great detail as opposed to zooming the reader along, including no sight descriptions at all. Today you'll return to *Owl Moon* and compare Yolen's choices to Smith's in "Gimmetheball" so your students will see that writers make purposeful choices to control the pace of their writing. For more information on pacing, see my book, *Fluent Writing* (2006).

8.2 | Books to Enjoy Today as First Reads

You need to prepare to discuss smell for tomorrow's sense of the day. I love "The smell of garbage bullies the air," from Karen Hesse's *Come On, Rain!* Interestingly, there are no descriptions related to the sense of smell in *Owl Moon*, which provides an opportunity for a discussion about purpose: Why did Yolen make that choice? *Oma's Quilt* by Paulette Bourgeois opens with the detail of smell and provides an opportunity to discuss how certain places, like your grandmother's house, have special, meaningful, memory-evoking smells.

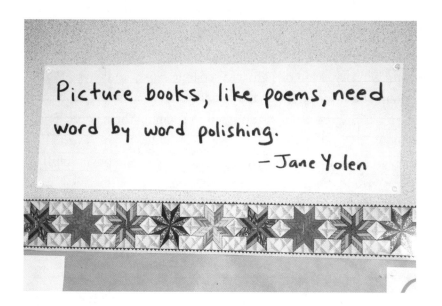

8.3 | Author Support

Jane Yolen has a lot to say about revision work. You could assign one or more students to search her Web site for a good quote. I like this particular one because it supports thinking across more than one genre.

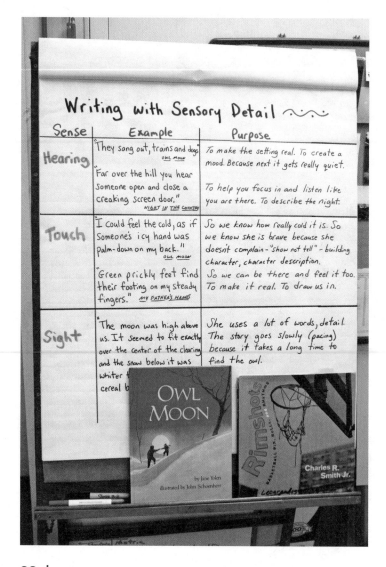

8.4 | Mini-Lesson: Exploring Sensory Details—Sight

Teaching point: Writers use sensory detail to draw in the reader; focus on sight. Depending on the text you've used, your discussions, and your students' own ideas, your chart might be filled in like this after your mini-lesson and discussion.

Return to *Owl Moon* for the sensory detail of sight. It's loaded, of course. The question you want to explore is *why*. I have found the best way to do that is to compare it with a piece with very few sight details.

Mini-Lesson: Exploring Sensory Details—Sight

Call to the carpet with notebooks and pencils: "Check yourselves."

Connect: "Writers, so far this week, we've looked closely at the sensory details of sound and touch in writing. We've been thinking about author's purpose both in where in the writing these senses are used and why a writer uses them. Today, we'll focus on sight."

Teach: "We know writers use sensory details to make their writing come alive for their readers. When you use the sensory detail of sight, you are creating images for your reader that can draw them into the piece. Visual imagery makes your writing powerful because your readers can imagine actually being there. But as we learned yesterday, writers are purposeful about where they will describe what things look like in great detail."

Explore: "I have two different texts here, *Owl Moon* and 'Gimmetheball.' Remember in 'Gimmetheball' we don't know if the basketball game takes place in a gym with polished hardwood floors or outdoors on an asphalt court. The writer doesn't tell us. Why not? In *Owl Moon*, almost every page has carefully crafted descriptions of what there is to see. Why?" [*Facilitate a discussion and record ideas. Your students should come to the understanding that the pace of these two pieces is very different; a lot of describing details for the reader slows a piece down. If they don't have it, give them the writer's word* pacing.]

Practice: "Let's practice this skill right now. Jane Yolen wrote in great detail about how things looked. Let's try that together right now. See how the sunlight is coming through our windows over there? Let's think of words that will create an image so someone who is not here can imagine just what that corner of our room looks like." [*Describe a part of your room orally or write it on a chart.*]

Link and excuse to write: "Just like our first two days this week, our writing time will be in two parts today. First we'll go outside and focus just on our sense of sight. Then we'll come back in and share our word choices. After a share, we'll look back in our notebooks to do some revision work and add the sensory detail of sight to our writing to a part where we want to slow it down."

After the observation part: Model looking through your own writing and thinking about a piece that would be appropriate to slow down by adding lots of descriptive imagery. Think out loud about entries or parts of entries that you are not adding to because you don't want to slow the pace. Do you need to review how to use the skipped line to fit the writing in, or use the opposite blank page?

Conferring

Be sure you are getting around to everyone, seeing four or so students per day. Continue to teach the strategies of thinking about purpose, thinking about the reader, and using mentor text.

8.5 | Closure: Sharing Writing and Grow Vocabulary Chart

Record vocabulary and share the process of deciding where a piece should be slowed down with imagery and why, and share what the revised piece sounds like with the slower pace.

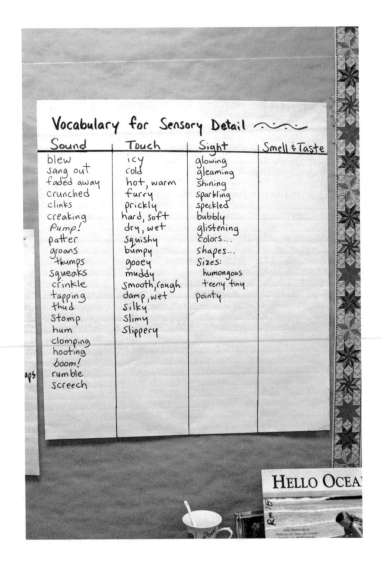

8.6 | Close Imitation

When a student writer produces writing that is not plagiarized, but sounds very similar to a bit of mentor text, that is called *close imitation*. It's what you hope for. It means students are making progress toward absorbing the sound of good writing. When they are influenced by many authors and then they add their own "voice," they will produce good writing that will sound individual but not unique. Every writer can tell you what other writers have influenced them most. In my class, I always have at least one boy who loves the sound of "Gimmetheball" and tries it out in his own writing.

and I thought we were not going to play because it was raining but then we drove to camlble commuite setter and we played I passed it to yanr. he past it back. I passed it to preston. it hit the post. and went out. after that I felt rain diping. across my face. then they kicked it and wen't to me I passed it to daren. he passed it to cristafur. he passed it to me. and I scorcd. and I could smell sweet vitory and it was my brothers birthday and that why it was my happies day don't forget to tell your friends

Do it:
~~Try it~~ Practice writing what you see/observe.
- OR -
Revise using imagery to slow the pace.

8.7 | Homework Do-It

I like to give a choice to differentiate and to honor those students who were able to grasp the pacing strategy and want to give it a try.

Exploring Sensory Details—
Smell

Overview

Details related to smell are used sparingly by writers, but they can be very powerful when crafted well. You are continuing your layered focus of learning about purpose. Why do writers make the choices they do?

9.1 | Chart Walls

Here are my reading and writing walls after Day 8 and before Day 9.

9.2 | Books to Enjoy Today as First Reads

Looking through my picture book collection, I find writing that uses the sense of taste is rare. The young narrator of *Come On, Rain!* pours a spoonful of sugar into her mouth, but Hesse doesn't linger there with description of the actual taste. Perhaps you'll find an example in your own collection of picture books. Instead, I read these books by Jane Yolen, and we practice listening for sensory vocabulary, which we will add to our sensory detail vocabulary chart.

I do know chapter books in which the author includes details about taste; for example, Roald Dahl's *Charlie and the Chocolate Factory*. And by now, we are a few days into Dahl's *Fantastic Mr. Fox*, so I do point out how Dahl spends time describing the taste of the cider that the characters enjoy so much.

To prepare for tomorrow, and as long as we are presenting a variety of genres to our students, you could decide to gather some examples from the functional writing genre of cookbooks—just for fun. The descriptive writing bits are concise and rich with an artful use of all the senses. It's a wonderful place to have a discussion about purpose. You can use bits from your favorite well-written cookbooks, or see what your school library has for kids.

Note about author support: At this point, I am happy with the quotes I have up on the wall. If you or your students find something wonderful and meaningful to support your work in progress, discuss and add it to the collection, being careful not to add too many. You could replace the ones that your students have internalized with new ones you find. You want all posted charts and quotes to be useful and used.

9.3 | Mini-Lesson: Exploring Sensory Details—Smell

Teaching point: Writers use sensory detail to draw in the reader; focus on smell. Depending on the text you've used, your discussion, and your students' own ideas, your chart might be filled in like this after your mini-lesson and discussion.

Sense	Example	Purpose
Hearing	"They sang out, trains and dogs" *OWL MOON*	To make the setting real. To create a mood. Because next it gets really quiet.
	"Far over the hill you hear someone open and close a creaking screen door." *NIGHT IN THE COUNTRY*	To help you focus in and listen like you are there. To describe the night.
Touch	"I could feel the cold, as if someone's icy hand was palm-down on my back." *OWL MOON*	So we know how really cold it is. So we know she is brave because she doesn't complain - "show not tell" - building character, character description.
	"Green prickly feet find their footing on my steady fingers." *MY FATHER'S HANDS*	So we can be there and feel it too. To make it real. To draw us in.
Sight	"The moon was high above us. It seemed to fit exactly over the center of the clearing and the snow below it was whiter than the milk in a cereal bowl." *OWL MOON*	She uses a lot of words, detail. The story goes slowly (pacing) because it takes a long time to find the owl.
Smell	"The smell of hot tar and garbage bullies the air..."	To pull us in. So we know how really hot, disgustingly hot it is. To slow the pace with detail.

Come On, Rain! BY Karen Hesse PICTURES BY Jon J Muth

Mini-Lesson: Exploring Sensory Details—Smell

Call to the carpet with notebooks and pencils: "Check yourselves."

Connect: "Writers, yesterday we focused on the sensory detail of sight and we revised our own writing to provide better visual imagery for our readers. Today, we'll focus on the sensory detail of smell."

Teach: "The sense of smell is not often used in writing. There is no description of smell in *Owl Moon* or in 'Gimmetheball,' for instance. Yesterday we read Karen Hesse's *Come On, Rain!* In one part she describes a smell of garbage that 'bullies the air.' Notice not just the smell but the great verb choice as well. *Oma's Quilt* opened with the sense of smell, but that was the only place the writer used that sense. Just as we've learned all week, writers are purposeful about when to add smell to their pieces. So that's our job now, to think about why."

Explore: "Let's look at *Come On, Rain!* and 'Gimmetheball' again. Why does 'Gimmetheball' not include descriptions of smell? Couldn't the writer have added the smell of the leather of the ball has it passed through the narrator's hands? Or maybe the smell of sweat or hot asphalt? Why doesn't he? Why does Hesse talk about the smell of the garbage?" [*Facilitate a discussion by revisiting pacing. Like yesterday, your students should come to understand that the pace of these two pieces is very different, and therefore a lot of details might slow the reader down. While Smith wants to stick with the fast action, Hesse wants us to know just how horribly hot it is; she wants to sharpen the focus and help slow the pace of the story.*]

Practice: "If we are going to add details about the sense of smell to our writing, we'll need to develop our writer's skills first by practicing writing about just what we smell. We'll go outside again today."

Link and excuse to write: "Our writing time will be in two parts today. First we'll go outside and focus just on our sense of smell. Then we'll come back in and share our word choices. After a share, we'll look back in our notebooks to do some revision work and add sensory details about smell to our writing."

After the observation: Model looking through your own writing and thinking about a piece that would be appropriate to slow down, pulling the reader in by adding details relating to smell. Think out loud about entries or parts of entries that you are not adding to because you don't want to slow the pace, or where it doesn't make sense. Review how to use the skipped line to fit the writing in, or use the opposite blank page.

9.4 | Closure: Sharing Writing and Growing the Vocabulary Chart

Share the process of deciding where a piece should be slowed down and sharpened with details about the sense of smell, and why. Record word choices.

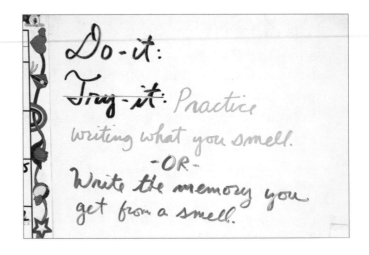

Vocabulary for Sensory Detail

Sound	Touch	Sight	Smell & Taste
blew	icy	glowing	a splat of mud
sang out	cold, cool	gleaming	a new car
faded away	hot, warm	shining	freshly cut wood
crunched	furry	sparkling	chocolate
clinks	prickly	speckled	sweet scent of sugar
creaking	hard, soft	bubbly	musty
pump!	dry, wet	glistening	reeky
patter	squishy	colors...	
groans	bumpy	shapes...	
thumps	gooey	Sizes:	
squeaks	muddy	humongous	
crinkle	smooth, rough	teeny tiny	
tapping	damp, wet		
thud	silky	pointy	
stomp	slimy	curled	
hum	slippery	squinty	
clomping	mushy	flutter	
hooting			
boom!			
rumble			
screech			
crackling			
snuffling			

HELLO OCEAN

9.5 | Homework Do-It

You can differentiate by offering a choice here similar to yesterday's.

Do-it:

~~Try-it:~~ Practice writing what you smell.
-OR-
Write the memory you get from a smell.

Wiggle-Room Day

Overview

You may have found you wanted to spend two days on one sense. If not, you can do an inquiry today into why writers do or don't choose to use the sensory detail of taste, or you could move on to Week 3.

If you decided to gather cookbooks yesterday for a discussion about the sense of taste today, then you could spend some time recording taste vocabulary from the cookbooks. I like to have out an assortment of food items on paper plates for small groups to taste. I keep in mind the diversity of food cultures when I make my food choices. (I check for food allergies first.) Have your students practice trying to put into words what they are tasting. Remind them to use their jot page to record any strong memories evoked by the flavors they're experiencing.

10.1 | Reading Workshop Supporting Work

As always, coordinated and supportive reading work you do outside of your writing workshop will extend, deepen, and strengthen your students' understanding and improve their writing and reading skills. Over the next two weeks, you'll be taking them through the writing process to a Quick Publish. Therefore, it's a good idea to preload this work by looking at genre and text structure in a simplified way appropriate for your grade level, because your students will need to choose a structure for their finished piece. Take the books out of your genre mentor basket and chart the genres and structures in a basic way that makes sense for your class and grade level. I like using a variety of Yolen's books to show that one author can write in many different genres, using different structures for different audiences and purposes.

Choosing, Developing, and Drafting an Idea for Publishing

Four Goals

- Continue building a safe and productive writing community

- Continue the writing process

- Develop the understanding—writing has structure

- Generate lots of thinking, talk, and writing

Overview of Week 3

Remember, your launch is not meant to produce brilliant pieces of writing. You have done no real deep study into craft or structure or pacing, but you have set the stage for that awareness to develop and for deeper units of study throughout the year.

Your launch is meant to set up your rituals and routines, make students feel safe to explore meaningful topics, share and write a lot, understand the basic elements of all good writing, and then do a Quick Publish to learn the steps of the writing process. This week starts the focus on that Quick Publish. You will introduce the planning, drafting, and response steps of the writing process, including choosing a meaningful seed idea, growing that idea, and then moving that idea from notebook to draft. You will be creating writing process charts that you can return to all year in every subsequent unit of study.

Your students will also be choosing a structure for their seed ideas. They will most likely write a personal narrative, but some students may write poetry, a descriptive piece, or an informational piece. It depends on what your students have taken an interest in and what kind of mentor texts you are using for text structure. You'll want your students to come to see that mentor texts are where writers go to envision how their own piece might look, to get ideas for structure while considering audience and purpose. You started focusing on this work last Friday, or earlier, with a structure chart appropriate for your grade level (see photo 10.1).

In your read-alouds and your reading work, you will be continuing work you started last week—reading some of the same books from the first two weeks but this time asking students to listen and think about structure. To preempt any "but we've already read that book" comments, you can say something like, "Writers study the same book/poem/piece of writing many times, noticing and studying different things." If your tone is genuinely enthusiastic and curious, then your students will also be enthusiastic and curious every time you return to the same text to think more deeply about it.

Adjusting the Week for Yourself, Your Class, and Grade Level

As always, you will adjust the level of language in the scripted lessons for your grade level. You also need to consider at what level you will approach the aspect of structure this week. Remember, children of all ages can compare and contrast different writing structures when given clear examples, and then choose one they would like to imitate.

Suggestions for Supporting Work to Do in Your Reading Workshop

I begin work this week studying narrative story structure because many of my students are writing personal narratives in this launch, and I am planning a unit of study on narrative structures in writing after the launch.

Supporting Work for Your Language Use and Conventions Block

- Add to your spelling strategies and punctuation work as appropriate.

- Continue to have students self-edit in their notebooks every morning.

Supporting Daily Homework and Homework Share

There is never enough time to write in class. As you begin to move toward publishing, writing homework becomes an opportunity for students to spend extra time on their writing projects by continuing the work of the day. I explain this, and stop writing Try-Its on the board until after this unit. I still check for completed writing homework in the morning, and we continue to share and edit. Some students will write entries unrelated to their writing projects, but most will use the extra time to advance their projects.

Choosing a Seed Idea

Overview

Your students (and you) now have a notebook filled with different ideas, many jots and many long-writes, perhaps even some simple poems inspired by your outdoor sensory observation time. I usually have at least one student who, in addition to memories and stories, has written a lot of information about a passionate interest such as snakes. Your student writers should understand that they have not simply been drafting in their notebooks, but rather collecting ideas, exploring ideas, and developing ideas, unified by the fact that all they have written has meaning for them. Some or many of their entries may sound like narratives, poems, descriptive or informational pieces, but they are not drafts just yet. This is an important point because you want a thoughtful switch from notebook to draft paper, not just copying over.

Before you start: It's Monday; would your students benefit from a review of rituals and routines? Where have you noticed weaknesses, and what do you need to review?

11.1 | Chart Walls

Here are my chart walls after Week 2 and before starting Week 3.

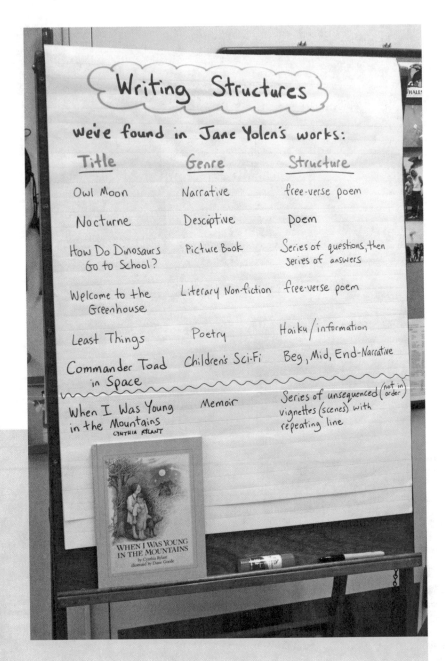

The chart reads:

Writing Structures

we've found in Jane Yolen's works:

Title	Genre	Structure
Owl Moon	Narrative	free-verse poem
Nocturne	Desciptive	poem
How Do Dinosaurs Go to School?	Picture Book	Series of questions, then series of answers
Welcome to the Greenhouse	Literary Non-fiction	free-verse poem
Least Things	Poetry	Haiku/information
Commander Toad in Space	Children's Sci-Fi	Beg, Mid, End-Narrative
When I Was Young in the Mountains CYNTHIA RYLANT	Memoir	Series of unsequenced (not in order) vignettes (scenes) with repeating line

11.2 |
Books to Enjoy Today as Focused Second Reads

Return to a previously read book, but focus on structure this time. *When I Was Young in the Mountains* by Cynthia Rylant is a good choice because of its atypical structure: a series of unsequenced vignettes, held together by a repeating line. Tell your students that on this second read you want them to listen for the structure. Then, when they see it doesn't fit narrative, poetry, or descriptive, add the vignette structure to the structure chart you started last week. Someone may want to use this structure for his or her finished piece. I've seen it done well, in a launch, by an average third-grade boy, way back when I didn't really know how to teach writing other than to say, "Use a mentor text!" (The entire text of that student's writing is in my first book, *Fluent Writing* [2006].)

11.3 | Author Support

Go to the Roald Dahl Web site and play his answer to the interview question, "How do you get the ideas for your stories?" Then post a piece of his answer, such as I have here, being sure to include the "seed" part, to refer to in your mini-lesson today.

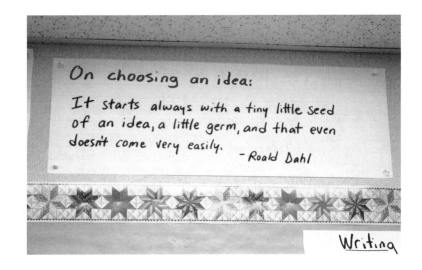

11.4 | Unit of Study Calendar

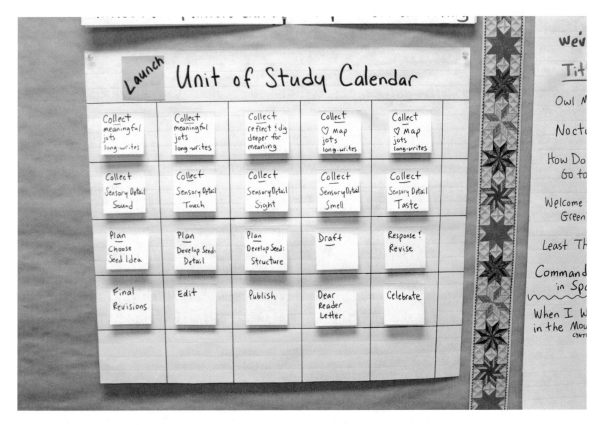

You can introduce this unit-planning calendar anytime during in this launch unit. In all my subsequent units of the year, it comes out on the first day. But for my launch unit with the focus on building community and building a solid understanding of writing for our writing workshop, I prefer to wait until now, using it to review what we've accomplished so far and to see what is ahead. Plan to share this calendar after you gather students on the carpet as visual support for the "connect" part of your mini-lesson. Then find a permanent spot for it on your chart wall.

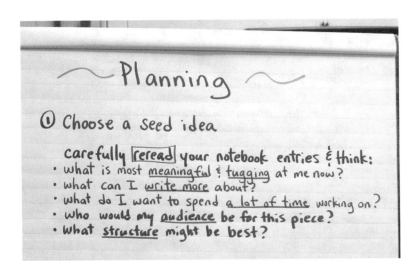

Teaching point: Writers thoughtfully choose a seed idea from all their collected ideas to develop into a finished piece.

Mini-Lesson: Choosing an Idea

Call students to the carpet, empty-handed: "Check yourselves."

Connect: "Writers, we've done so much over the last two weeks. We've looked at all the basic elements of good writing. We've also done work in conventions and spelling to support our writing work, and you've been practicing those convention skills by editing every morning in your writer's notebooks. Wow! We've accomplished so much!

"Now comes the next exciting part. We're going to use all this good work we've done and create one finished piece of writing using the writing process. All of our names have been in the *Collect* part of the wheel [*see photo P.19*] since the start of school. The next step on our process wheel after *Collect* is *Plan*. Planning starts with choosing an idea."

Explain: "After doing a lot of collecting, writers will choose an idea, a seed of an idea, as Roald Dahl calls it, to develop and then draft, edit, and publish. [*Point to Dahl quote and/or play his interview answer.*] Choosing a seed idea is no easy task; it requires a lot of rereading and thinking."

Model: "I am going to model choosing an idea that I would like to work more on. Calling it a seed idea is a wonderful way to think about how, after we choose our idea, we will nurture it and help it grow into a finished piece. Please have a look at this chart here and see what I—and you—need to do.

"As I look at this chart I see I need to carefully *reread* my writer's notebook. And I need to think carefully about these other important things."

Remember your modeling is very powerful. If you zip through the process, they will, too. So take your time without taking too much of theirs. Model going through the chart thoughtfully, one point at a time. Model thinking about different kinds of possibilities: an idea that is just a jot, an idea that is a few pages long, pieces of several entries that could be combined, a piece of one entry. Also model imagining the best genre and structure for your idea. Then choose one thing and model checking the list again. I advise you to choose an idea that is kid-friendly, perhaps something that happened to you when you were their age. Finally, it is very important to model choosing something manageable for your Quick Publish. Remind them that Jane Yolen wrote about finding an owl one night, not "My Life on the Farm." Lucy Calkins calls this choosing a seed, not the whole watermelon. If you have students who want to write about an amusement park (that does seem to be a meaningful topic for many), encourage them to write in great sensory detail about one ride instead of "My Day at the Amusement Park." *Roller Coaster* by Marla Frazee would be a good mentor text to have available, especially for younger students.

Practice: "Today, when you get back to your seats and your notebooks, you will have some very important work to do—choosing your seed idea. First we'll do a turn-and-talk. Please tell your partner, using the chart, what you will be doing. When you are finished talking, I'll answer any questions before you go."

Link and excuse to write: "Our writing time today will look different because we will be rereading our notebooks and carefully thinking. You may use sticky notes to mark possible ideas until you narrow one down. Each of you should plan on explaining your decision and thinking process at our closure, which will be a little bit longer than usual so everyone has time to share. I would like to encourage you to talk with each other about the seed ideas that you are considering. Please use the language of the chart to help you in your conversations. Talking about a big decision helps you make a good decision. If you are very sure about your seed idea choice before it is time for closure, please write more about your idea, or read mentor texts that will help you imagine a structure for your finished piece. If you do not choose a seed idea by closure, don't worry—careful thinking takes time. If you know what to do, look at me, and I'll excuse you."

11.6 | Peer Conferring

When I have a big decision to make, talking about it helps. You cannot get around to all the students who need to talk through their decision, so you especially want to encourage peer conferring today. Encourage students to listen to each other's ideas and to help each other using the language of the chart. Of course, we all have our different processes, and some students may prefer to think alone.

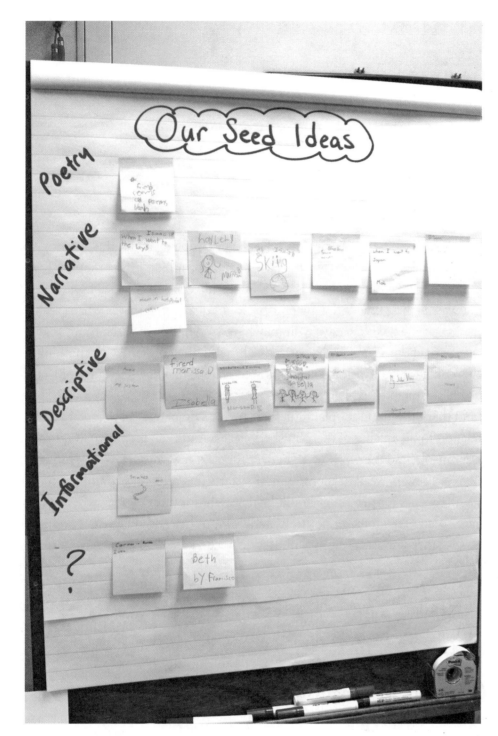

11.7 | Closure: Seed Idea Chart

A chart like this is for commitment and accountability. It also helps you keep track of who is working on what, and you can use it to form small groups of children with similar structures, topics, or other needs for conferring. And I have found that when students can see their peers' seed ideas, they are eager to help one another with suggestions about which mentor texts to use for detail or structure ideas.

Growing the
Seed Idea

Overview

The writing process is a journey of discovery. Speak openly about this, sharing your own experiences in choosing your seed idea. For example, "First I thought I would write about the day the family dog died, but as I lived with the idea for awhile, I remembered it was the first time I saw my dad cry, and I discovered that is what I really want to write about." Over the next few days, you may have students change their minds about the seed idea they've chosen, and this is perfectly all right—it shows they are thinking deeply. When students come to you to ask for permission to change to a new seed idea or to tell you their new choice, ask them to explain their reasoning.

I have found that the amount of planning that students do before they actually draft has a direct correlation to the quality of their finished pieces. And I tell them so. I want them to know the reasoning behind the work we'll do over the next few days. However, too much planning before drafting (a week or more) typically starts to scatter and confuse a student writer's focus. A few days for planning should be just right for most of your writers. This planning time also gives them the opportunity to live with their idea before committing it to a draft, making sure they are really happy with their choice.

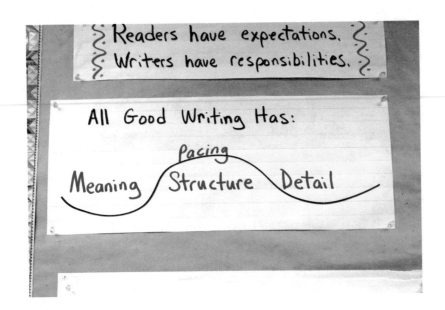

12.1 | "All Good Writing Has" Chart

This sums up all that we've studied in our launch and is the basis for all future units. I refer to it all year; place yours in a permanent spot.

～ Planning ～

① Choose a seed idea

> carefully [reread] your notebook entries & think:
> - what is most meaningful & tugging at me now?
> - what can I write more about?
> - what do I want to spend a lot of time working on?
> - who would my audience be for this piece?
> - what structure might be best?

② Develop your seed idea

- dig for deeper meaning w/web
- sketch to remember details
- •
- •
- •
- •
- •

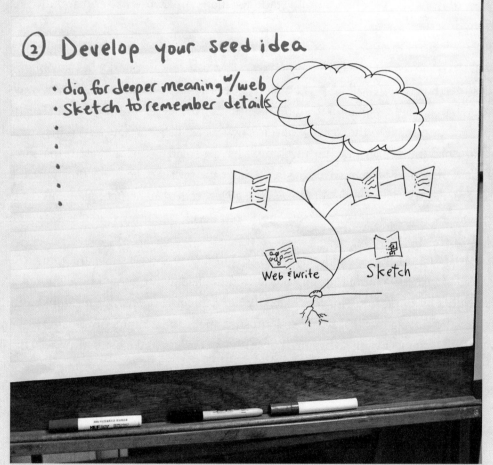

Web & write   Sketch

12.2 | Mini-Lesson: Make a Sketch—Grow Your Seed Idea

Teaching point: Writers develop their ideas before they draft.

Mini-Lesson: Make a Sketch—Grow Your Seed Idea

Call to carpet, empty-handed: "Check yourselves."

Connect: "Writers, yesterday most of you selected an idea that you would like to take through the writing process. You were thoughtful about choosing one idea out of your notebook. Today we are still in the step before drafting, or the planning stage. Planning is where you choose and develop your seed idea, before you draft. Drafting is what you do when you move your focused idea out of your notebook and onto yellow draft paper. We are not quite ready for that yet because writers carefully plan before they draft."

Explain: "We will be planning for a few days before we draft. Doing this planning work before you draft will help you make better drafts. There are many, many ways to develop your idea. I have a few on this chart for us, and over the year we'll learn more and add them to the "leaves" of this drawing that shows how a seed idea grows to a finished piece. To guide our thinking, I have a small permanent chart that sums up our work and will help us always remember the basics of good writing and all that our readers expect. [*Point to "All Good Writing Has" chart.*] As writers plan and develop their pieces, they remember to ask themselves, 'Do I have all my reader is expecting?'"

Model: "I am going to model for you my thinking process. First, I am going to use this 'All Good Writing Has' chart as a kind of checklist. I know I have chosen an idea with a lot of meaning for me. I already did a 'digging deeper for meaning' web on this idea during our first week, so I am sure about the meaning. But I am not sure how I will write it. I want to be sure I give my reader lots of details, sensory details. I wrote some last night. I know I need more, but I want to be sure they are purposeful. I am not sure of a structure yet, but I think I want it to be a descriptive piece. I don't know yet if I want the pace to be fast or slow. Hmm, all of that is a lot to think about. I need a strategy to help me think more about what I want to write and how I want to write it. The strategy I am going to use and model for you is called 'make a detailed drawing.' As I am sketching and adding lots of details and thinking out loud for you, I want you to think about what would be a good person, place, or thing for you to sketch today with a lot of detail to help you develop your seed idea."

Sketch in front of the class, thinking out loud as you go. Make a point about sketching important parts, people, or places, not just any random thing. Have the drawing help you clarify the meaning. Think out loud about how drawing in such detail is helping you remember so many details. As you are developing your seed idea through this sketch, model how you are determining whether the pacing will be fast or slow. Finally, talk about focusing on your structure choice. This year, as I was drawing in front of my students, I modeled changing my idea about my structure. I decided that it wasn't enough just to describe that mean music teacher in that dreary room; what I needed was a narrative structure, because I wanted to tell what happened before and after that moment. I no longer had a descriptive piece, I had a story with a beginning, middle, and end.

Be careful what you model. Don't get too ambitious by trying to tackle a big writing project. Time is short. This is a Quick Publish, and students need to be able to finish their pieces on time and be pleased with the results. I also modeled thinking about the publishing deadline and sticking with a seed, not a watermelon.

Practice: "Please turn to the person next to you and say what you will be sketching today in detail to help you develop your idea."

Link and excuse to write: "At closure today, we'll talk and share our sketches and how they helped us focus and develop our ideas. If you finish a detailed sketch and there is still time before closure, do some writing in your notebook off of your sketch. If you know what to do, look at me and I'll excuse you."

Conferring

Check your writing process wheel for the status of your class. Do you need to meet with a small group of students who are still struggling with choosing a seed idea? I prefer groups of no more than four at a time. After gathering them at the group conference table, I start with the strongest student. I assist this child while the others listen. I do not ask students in a small group what they are working on, as I would in an individual conference. They are all there for one common purpose, one common teaching point that I have determined they need. I finish with the weakest or most confused student last. He or she will have heard the point I am making three times already, which is usually a big help.

Closure

Make this a time for students to talk and share their sketches. Through talking and sharing, they will continue to develop their seed ideas. Remember your tone—enthusiasm is contagious.

13.1 | Mini-Lesson: Studying Text Structure—Growing Your Seed Idea

Teaching point: Writers develop their ideas before they draft.

Conferring

Again, you cannot get around to everyone. That is why you have been encouraging talking with peers from the beginning. By now, your students should be comfortable thinking deeply with others about writing. And they should not be dependent on you. However, some do have special needs. Is there a small group of students you should gather who would benefit from scaffolding?

Mini-Lesson: Studying Text Structure— Growing Your Seed Idea

Call to the carpet, empty-handed: "Check yourselves."

Connect: "Writers, yesterday you did some detailed sketching to help you develop your idea. As we talked and shared at our closure, we noticed our ideas are starting to take shape. Let's take one more day before we draft and develop our ideas a little further. Today we'll be focusing on choosing a mentor text or texts to help us."

Explain: "During this launch unit we have enjoyed many different kinds of books. We have quite a collection in our unit-of-study basket, including some poetry, some narratives, some descriptive and some informational writing. We know writers read a lot because reading helps with their writing; it helps with word choice, pacing, sensory detail, ways to show a reader why the writing is meaningful, and structures for the writing. Using mentors to help us imagine our structures is what we'll focus on today."

Model: "I am going to model for you my thinking process. I am going look through some of these books and get some ideas on how to structure my writing."

Differentiate: "Writers, I know some of you have chosen a mentor to use already and you have a very clear idea about your structure. You may wish to develop your idea in other ways before we draft tomorrow. There are other 'leaves' to choose from."

Practice: "Please turn to the person next to you and tell him or her what you will be doing today to help you develop your idea. Who will be studying mentors today? Who will be doing this work with a partner? By themselves?"

   You can get a sense of how many students have committed to trying the teaching point in your mini-lessons by asking for a show of hands. Give some wait time and more hands will rise.

Link and excuse to write: "At closure today, we'll share our chosen mentor texts and structures. If you know what to do, look at me, and I'll excuse you."

Day 14

Drafting

Overview

This is the big day to move all that work out of the notebook and onto yellow draft paper. Writers are individuals, so be sure to give them some choices. Make the drafting chart ahead of time. It's very specific so students can refer to the chart.

Before you start the lesson, update the Our Seed Ideas chart. Some students may have changed their minds and have a new seed idea. Ask them to explain their reasoning using the criteria on the Planning chart, and honor their choices. Also check to see whether genre choices have changed.

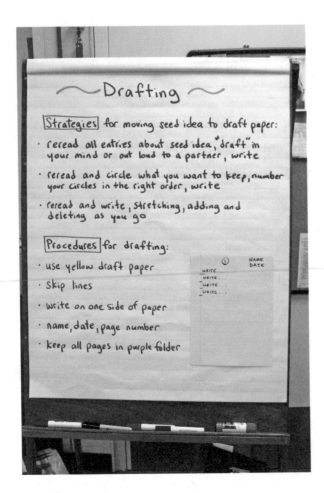

14.1 | Mini-Lesson: Moving From Notebook to Draft Paper

Teaching point: Writers thoughtfully move their ideas from notebook to draft. For this mini-lesson be sure to model the process that works best for you. Remember, these will be fairly simple writing pieces, maybe only a page, so your students should be able to draft them in one day, especially after all the thinking and growing of seed ideas that they've done in these past days. Keep the mini-lesson brief so they can get busy drafting.

Mini-Lesson: Moving From Notebook to Draft Paper

Call to the carpet, empty-handed: "Check yourselves."

Connect: "Writers, we've spent a few days developing our seed ideas. Now it's time to pull all that good thinking together and draft."

Explain: "There are two parts to this chart I have prepared for you: the strategies part and the procedures part. [*Review the procedures part first.*] Is everyone clear on how to draft on the yellow draft paper? Now for strategies. As I read these out loud, think to yourselves about which strategy will work best for you."

Practice: "Please turn to the person next to you and tell him or her which strategy you think will work best for you."

Link and excuse to write: "At closure today, we'll share out our processes for moving our seed idea out of our notebooks and creating a draft, and tell how it went. If you know what to do, look at me, and I'll excuse you."

Conferring

Be careful not to return to the same student you saw the day before. Make an announcement to the class if you need to. Continue to foster independence not by correcting drafts, but by guiding students to charts and mentor texts.

Closure

Gather students on the carpet. Share processes and be sure to point out how well they did with such a difficult task. Talk about how difficult but rewarding all this hard work can be.

Responding

Overview

Y ou are doing a Quick Publish so students can experience every step of the writing process. Successful peer response groups and partnerships require a lot of teaching. I suggest making responding a focus of a future unit of study. For now, a one-day focus will do.

Before this lesson begins, I show the photo Jane Yolen has on her Web site of herself and the other writers she regularly meets with, and I read a bit of what she has to say about the importance of getting feedback.

You'll have to make this chart ahead of time. It's very specific so students can follow it on their own anytime today or next week, leaving you free to confer.

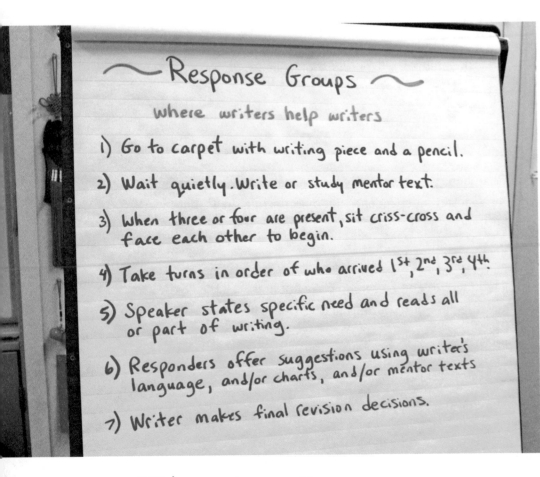

~ Response Groups ~

where writers help writers

1) Go to carpet with writing piece and a pencil.

2) Wait quietly. Write or study mentor text.

3) When three or four are present, sit criss-cross and face each other to begin.

4) Take turns in order of who arrived 1st, 2nd, 3rd, 4th.

5) Speaker states specific need and reads all or part of writing.

6) Responders offer suggestions using writer's language, and/or charts, and/or mentor texts

7) Writer makes final revision decisions.

15.1 | Mini-Lesson: Response Groups

Teaching point: Writers get feedback from other writers to improve their writing.

Mini-Lesson: Response Groups

Call to the carpet, empty-handed: "Check yourselves."

Connect: "Writers, you've been working so hard. Most of you have completed your drafts, which brings you to the next part of the writing process—response. In a way, we've all been getting and giving responses to our ideas since the first day of school. You've been working well with partners, and I've had the pleasure of conferring with you. Today, we'll focus on something called *response groups*."

Explain: "This morning we looked at a photo of Jane Yolen and her response group. Not just friends of hers, but *writer* friends of hers. Writers help writers. Today, if you are ready, please try a response group. You don't have to have a finished draft—you can go to get help with what you have so far. It's good to get feedback from different people in class who are not your usual partners. If you would like to be part of a response group, follow the instructions and procedures on this chart. [*Review the premade chart.*] And remember, you make the choices on whether to make the revisions suggested in your response group or not."

Practice: "Please turn to the person next to you and tell him or her whether you plan to go a response group today, and what feedback you might be asking for."

Link and excuse to write: "At closure today, we'll share out how it went in the response groups and if anyone used feedback to make revisions to their drafts. If you know what to do, look at me, and I'll excuse you."

15.2 | Peer Conferring

These girls are not in what I would call a response group. They sit next to each other and often respond to each other's writing when needed.

Conferring

It would be helpful to sit near response groups today and offer positive feedback, pointing out what the students are doing well—referring to the chart for procedural guidance, asking for specific feedback, listening with interest, and offering suggestions using the language of writers.

15.3 | Response Group

These students left their seats and formed a group on the rug. They did not plan to meet, they simply wanted feedback, and as they arrived, the group formed until it was full— four students. You may want to have a maximum of three in younger grades.

Closure

This is hard work. Keep the energy up by getting obviously excited by your students' writing and how well they are learning to work with each other. If you find your time is tight for closure, do what I do on occasion: have a one-minute closure from their seats where you just ask for a thumbs-up or thumbs-down on how it went. You get a "temperature check," and they get maximum time for response groups and for writing.

Revise, Edit, Publish, Reflect, Celebrate

Four Goals

- Complete the writing process

- Develop the understanding—writers reflect on their writing

- Generate lots of thinking, talk, and writing

- Celebrate your safe and productive writing community

Overview of Week 4

This week wraps up your launch. There is still much to do: revise, edit, publish, write "Dear Reader" letters, and finally, celebrate.

This first piece of finished writing your students produce will likely not be long, but it should contain all the elements that you have studied in this launch unit to the best of their current abilities and understanding. To ensure this result, start the last week with a review of your unit of study chart, the writing process wheel to remind them to manage their time well, and your "All Good Writing Has" chart.

Adjusting the Week for Yourself, Your Class, and Grade Level

There is no wiggle-room day this week. If a student has taken on a writing project too big to complete in class, he or she will have to complete it at home. A deadline is a deadline, and this is an opportunity for students to learn to manage their time.

The timing of the "Dear Reader" letter day may be something you want to adjust. For some classes or grade levels, it may be more appropriate to have your celebration on Day 19 and your "Dear Reader" letter on the following day, because in the celebration, students can have a chance to practice ideas for their "Dear Reader" letters aloud.

When I first had students write "Dear Reader" letters, they wrote them after our celebration, and we displayed them next to finished pieces out in the hall (see photo 21.1). The first purpose of writing the letters was to have students articulate what they did well in their writing pieces. The second purpose was to give parents and others direction for what to notice in the piece, beyond any misspelled words.

My thinking has changed. The "Dear Reader" letter is highly personal and requires deep reflection. It should not just be about one or two points of writing craft. These letters, which sit next to the finished pieces at the celebration, provide an opportunity for students to think deeply about their writing and to make our celebration more meaningful.

You'll need to decide on the best order for Day 19 and Day 20 for your class and grade level.

Suggestions for Supporting Work to Do in Your Reading Workshop

As I enter the last week of any writing unit of study, I begin immersion for the next writing genre in my reading workshop. This week we will continue looking at narrative writing structure and story elements.

Supporting Work for Your Language Use and Conventions Block

I use this as a review week with the explicit expectation that all we are reviewing should show in their finished pieces in writing workshop. It would be helpful to teach and/or review letter writing conventions in preparation for the "Dear Reader" letter writing on Day 19.

Supporting Daily Homework and Homework Share

As students are wrapping up their pieces this week, many will be taking them home. Remind them to take enough draft or publishing paper home with them. It's sad to see a child who ran out of time in class and then published at home on a piece of binder paper with holes. After the publishing deadline this week, I start Try-Its that relate to the next genre we will study. In addition, I use this week to start using as first reads whatever I'll be using in my mini-lessons in my next unit of study.

Making Final
Revisions

Overview

Although this day is dedicated to revision, your students have practiced revision work already, so it should not seem like a new idea, or an isolated process, or something only to be considered on "revision day." Therefore, you could call this day "final revision day."

Author Support

You have two revision quotes up already. You or your students could search for more from a favorite author, or simply refer again to the quotes you already have.

16.1 |
Chart Walls

Here are my chart walls after Week 3 and before starting Week 4.

16.2 | Moving Through the Process

We have the class rule that every student moves only his or her own name tag around the process wheel. Explain to your students that they may be moving clockwise or counterclockwise, depending on where they are in the recursive writing process. A room full of diverse learners will not all be moving through the writing process at the same speed. But because the launch unit has a Quick Publish, students don't have as much time to spread out. They will be moving around the wheel more in sync now than in any future unit of study. What is unchangeable is your publishing deadline. Stick with it so your young writers have the opportunity to learn time management. The beauty of this chart is that it provides you with a quick visual. You see where everyone is and you can make decisions about gathering a small group of stragglers, or allowing some extra time, perhaps in your reading workshop, to publish pieces. Early publishers should move on to Collect again.

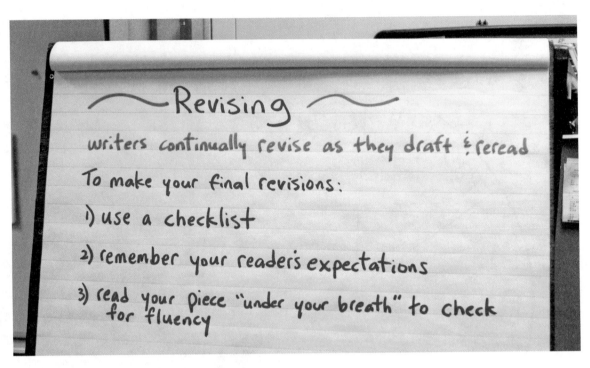

16.3 | Mini-Lesson: Final Revisions

Teaching point: When you are checking for final revisions, keep your reader in mind.

Mini-Lesson: Final Revisions

Call to the carpet, with drafts and a pencil: "Check yourselves."

Connect: "Writers, we are nearing the end of our unit. [*Point to Unit of Study chart.*] Last week you all chose a seed idea from your notebooks. You developed your seed idea. You decided on a structure. You drafted, being sure to include sensory detail for your reader. Some of you decided to control the pace of your piece. Most of you got feedback from a partner or from your peers in a response group. Many of you have been making revisions."

Explain: "We know already that revision is a continual part of the writing process, but at some point, you find yourself up against a publishing deadline, just as we are now, and you have to make your final revisions. When you are making final revisions, it helps to use a checklist and to think about your responsibility to your reader's expectations." [*Point to that little permanent chart.*]

Model: "I'm going to model thinking about my reader. To help me, I'll use our 'All Good Writing Has' chart as a checklist to remind me again of what my reader expects. I am going to check for one thing at a time.

"First I'll check for structure. I decided to take my seed idea and write it in a simple narrative structure, and as I reread, I see I have a beginning, middle, and an end that moves through time. Check.

"I'll check for meaning next. Yes, I added a reflective comment, like the one Cynthia Rylant used at the end of *When I Was Young in the Mountains*, so my reader knows why this piece is important to me. Check.

"Now, I am going to check for detail, sensory detail that we worked so hard on. I want to be sure that I have pulled my reader into my piece. Yes, I have detailed descriptions of the room and the teacher, I have the sound of my shoes tapping on the linoleum, but I forgot to add the musty smell of the room, here, where I thought it would work best. I'll add a star here to remind me.

"Now for the last revision check, pacing. I want my piece to read slowly and smoothly. I need to reread it, but not silently in my head because I might accidentally skip over something bumpy. When your pacing is smooth, your writing will have a nice flow to it. You can listen and check for that flow if you read it out loud. Watch and listen while I model reading 'under my breath.' Oops, I caught something here—this part doesn't read smoothly, so I think I'll add a bit here and change this sentence there . . . now I need to back up and reread under my breath again."

Practice: "Now it's your turn to try reading under your breath. Our classroom should sound like a humming murmur. Go. Yes, that is how it should sound. Raise your hand to share what you caught that is missing, or that doesn't read smoothly and you will need to revise."

Link and excuse to write: "Now, when you get back to your seats, think of your reader, go through our checklist, and finally, as a last check for smooth pacing, read under your breath to hear how your piece sounds. At closure today, we'll share your process. We will talk about how the checklist worked for you and how the reading and rereading under your breath worked for you—and what revisions you made and why. If you know what to do, look at me, and I'll excuse you."

Conferring

Remember to build more independence, not less. It's hard to do that, especially today, because you just want to jump in and correct their writing. Strategies to teach may sound like a repeat of the mini-lesson. "Writers reread to hear if the writing sounds smooth. Let me hear you read under your breath. Where does it not sound quite right? What kinds of revisions might make this part read smoothly?" You may also be conferring with students still finishing their drafts. Direct them to the vocabulary charts and mentor. Resist telling them what to add or how to finish.

Mid-Workshop Teach

Usually children have no problem coming up with a title: *My Best Friend, My First Bike, My Best Day Ever.* But if you see some long titles that sound more like a first sentence, you could make a note of it and do a mini-lesson on titles in your next unit, or decide to do a quick lesson on title revision right now: "Excuse me, writers. I am noticing some of you have titles that sound like a sentence, not a title. You may want to include your title in your final revision work today. Please notice all our mentors have fairly short titles, not a sentence." Hold up *Owl Moon* and make up a terrible title. Say something like "The First Time I Saw an Owl With My Pa" or whatever closely imitates what they have as titles. *Roller Coaster* becomes "My Favorite Ride at the Amusement Park." You get the idea. So will they.

Closure: Sharing the Process of Today's Work

Discuss the process. Lots of talk is important. Refer back to the "All Good Writing Has" chart to validate students' processes and celebrate their careful thinking and choices.

Homework note: You may want to remind your students that they should not be getting help at home, except for asking a parent how to spell a word. Tell them to tell their parents that the teacher said so. I have seen pieces come back from home completely changed by parents who did not understand the foundational work being done in class or the importance of the child finding his or her own writer's voice.

Doing the Final Edit

Overview

Sometimes the line between revision and editing work is blurred, such as when a writer revises conventions to make new meaning. You can look more deeply into this with your students over the course of the year. For now, help them understand that a final edit is when you apply all the work you've done in the Language Use and Conventions (word work) part of your day. Tell them you will hold them accountable for whatever conventions have been studied so far in the year, no more or less. You'll add to your editing checklist, and their responsibilities as student writers, as the year goes on. At this point in the year, I expect students to understand the use of capitals and periods and to spell high-frequency words correctly.

You might choose to have just an editing chart or make an editing checklist to hand out. You can have students update it as you teach more conventions, and keep it in their writing folder. If you have discovered through your assessments and conferences that certain children have special editing needs, then you help those students individualize their editing checklists. I prefer a chart and a lot of practice, because I have found, when given an editing sheet, students will simply check off the items to edit without much attention to their actual piece.

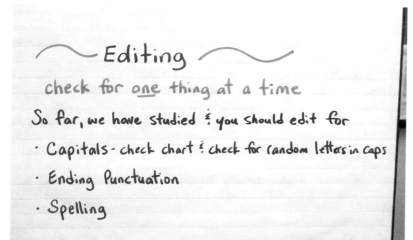

17.1 |
Mini-Lesson: Editing

Teaching point: When doing a final edit, edit for ONE thing at a time.

Mini-Lesson: Editing

Call to the carpet, with drafts and a pencil: "Check yourselves."

Connect: "Writers, you've all been working so hard and your pieces are sounding wonderful! It is time to make the final preparations for publishing. You want your draft to be the best it can be so your reader can enjoy your wonderful writing and not be distracted by errors."

Explain: "Editing is actually very complicated. There is so much to check for, and it is easy to read right over errors. Therefore, when editing, writers carefully focus on *one* thing at a time."

Model: "I'm checking the editing chart here. I am going through my entire piece, checking first for periods and then for capitals. The last things to check for are misspelled words. Reading word by word backwards is a strategy you could use."

Practice: "Now it's your turn to try. Choose one thing only and practice reading just for that."

Link and excuse to write: "Now it's time to return to your seats and finish editing. If you are finished early, you may offer assistance to a classmate. At closure we'll share how it went, checking for one thing at a time."

Conferring

I no longer assist with content at this point. We are out of time. I explain I am the editor-in-chief. I expect them all to make their best effort to edit their pieces well on their own. If they would like an editing conference, they should put out a green tag, and green tags today are only for editing conferences. When I sit down with them, I'll ask what editing they've done, and then I'll do a final check with my blue pen, circling misspelled words for them to look up. I use common editing marks: a slash to make a capital into lower case, three little underlines to make a lower case into a capital, and so on.

Publishing

Overview

Publishing is a process that must be taught. It's not as simple as just copying over neatly onto a clean piece of paper. What sort of look for these finished pieces is grade-level appropriate for your class? Would they like to do a little illustrating along the edges, or on a cover, or just present the piece on plain lined paper? Do you have a computer lab you'd like to use?

Conferring

I typically finish editing conferences on this day.

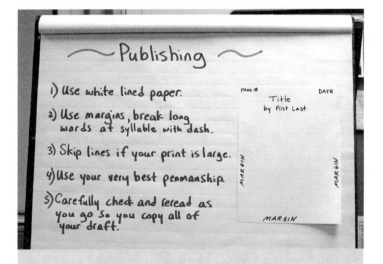

18.1 | Mini-Lesson: Publishing

Teaching point: Writers publish their pieces with great care and effort. Gather your students on the carpet as usual. Have a premade chart that explains what you expect. Whatever you decide for the look of your finished pieces, remember there are a few common points to teach:

- Use mentor texts to explain the conventions of writing a title, and that "by" on the author line is not capitalized.

- When using standard lined paper, ask the children to consider the size and legibility of their handwriting and then decide whether to skip lines or not.

- Teach margins, all four of them, especially the bottom one. Hold up any published text as an example.

Writing the
"Dear Reader"
Letter

Overview

This is a wonderful and important piece of all your units. This is where writers have a chance to talk to their readers about what they've written, about the choices they've made and struggles they've had. It's where your student writers have a chance to reflect on their hard work and solidify their learning.

You may want to photocopy samples of "Dear Reader" letters to make available for your students to study.

19.1 | Mini-Lesson: The "Dear Reader" Letter

Teaching point: Writers reflect on their writing.

Mini-Lesson: The "Dear Reader" Letter

Call to carpet, empty-handed: "Check yourselves."

Connect: "Writers, yesterday you worked hard and finished publishing your pieces, and now we've come to a very special day."

Explain: "Writers think and reflect about their own writing, and often they write down their reflections to share with their readers in what is called a 'Dear Reader' letter. I have two examples for you. The first is by Mary Pope Osborne, who includes 'Dear Reader' letters in the front of her Magic Tree House series books. The second one is from *If You Hopped Like a Frog* by David M. Schwartz. As I read these to you, please listen for how the writer is talking to you and begin thinking about how your 'Dear Reader' letter will sound."

Practice: "What might you put in your letter? Please think quietly to yourself, and then we'll have a few people share out."

Link and excuse to write: "At closure we'll be sharing some of our letters. I am going to write mine now as well."

Closure

This letter is very individual to each student writer's journey, but you will hear and can point out common threads that bind your community together.

Celebrating

Overview

The big day at last! What makes sense for you and your class? At subsequent celebrations throughout the year, I invite parents, sometimes other classrooms (especially with poetry) or our younger buddy class to hear and share narratives and informational picture books. There are so many ways to make your celebration meaningful by sharing polished writing.

I just received this e-mail from Libby James-Pasby, an extraordinary fourth- and fifth-grade teacher in the Oak Grove School District:

> By the way, on Friday we used the "comments to the writer" sheet with four upper-grade classes at the same time! I was worried that with that many students (140!) in one place they might feel overwhelmed and rush through each piece and not leave detailed comments. It really worked out nicely. The energy in the room was so focused . . . it was totally silent as all of these kids spent time with each piece that they read. They left really great comments for each other. Oh how I do love a good writing celebration!

I love a good celebration, too. And I am thinking now of how to pull off a big one later this school year, like Libby has done. But for the launch, we like to have a closed celebration. To celebrate not just the writing, but what we have become—a powerful and close writing community.

This is your day to celebrate all the hard work over the last 19 days. Food and drink are a normal part of human celebrations, and I include refreshments in the last ten minutes or so of the hour. But mostly, although they think they are celebrating the whole hour, the students are still working. They are continuing to use, absorb, and internalize writers' terms. They are thinking. They are reflecting.

20.1 | The Layout of the Room

Each child gets ready, placing his or her finished piece on the desk next to a "Comments to the Writer" paper filled in with the title (or "untitled"), date, and student's name.

20.2 | Author's Chair

I borrow a tall one to get them up high and place it at the front of the room. One student at a time sits to read. First the student tells us two things that he or she is really proud of and wants us to listen for in the writing. Then, the student reads, the class applauds, and positive comments are made. Teacher and/or students confirm that the two things the student is most proud of are in the writing and well done.

20.3 | Readers' Comments Sheet

After all have shared, the class rotates around the room, with each person leaving three to five thoughtful writerly comments for each published piece. I make comments, as well. In the future, so will parents who attend. The writing will stay at school, so the comments are the one thing that goes home for the parents to see and enjoy.

20.4 | Food and Drink

I teach my students the proper way to make a toast. And I hear things like, "To my writing partner, for helping me with my word choices," or "To Cynthia Rylant, for helping me craft my piece," or simply "To our writing!"

After the Launch
Displaying Student Work

Here are a few ideas for displaying your students' writing throughout the year.

21.1 | Writing Wall

Writing is meant to be shared. All around our school, writing from every student in every classroom is displayed. Children from other classrooms and parents stop by and read writing on the writing walls.

21.2 | Writing Piece and "Dear Reader" Letter

The "Dear Reader" letters direct the reader's attention to what the writer was working on in his or her piece.

21.3 | Student Names

Students decorate a folded piece of construction paper cut between their first and last names.

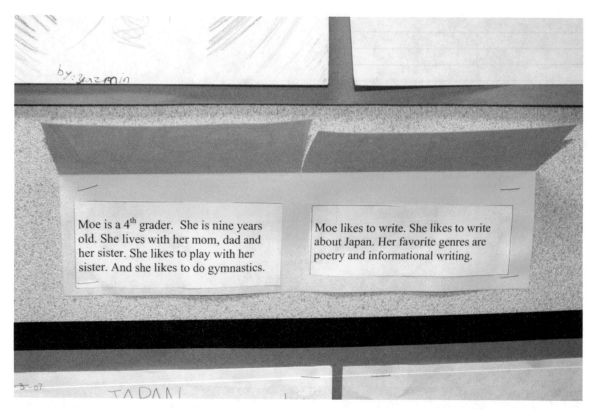

21.4 | About the Author

We study examples of "about the authors" as mentor texts. The children discover they must write about themselves in the third person. Not easy to do. I have typed these up so they look more professional and will last throughout the year.

And that wraps up the launch! Now you can take your community of writers on further adventures, learning to craft any genre of writing through close study of mentor texts.

Appendix

Launch Calendar at a Glance

Day 1	Day 2	Day 3	Day 4	Day 5
Establish Rituals and Routines Collect meaningful ideas from books	Establish Rituals and Routines Collect meaningful ideas from objects	Establish Rituals and Routines Dig deeper for meaning	Establish Rituals and Routines Create a source of meaningful ideas: Heart Map	Wiggle Room
Day 6	**Day 7**	**Day 8**	**Day 9**	**Day 10**
Sensory Detail: Sound	Sensory Detail: Touch	Sensory Detail: Sight	Sensory Detail: Smell	Wiggle Room or Sensory Detail: Taste
Day 11	**Day 12**	**Day 13**	**Day 14**	**Day 15**
Choose seed idea	Develop seed idea: Detail	Develop seed idea: Structure	Draft	Response and Revise
Day 16	**Day 17**	**Day 18**	**Day 19**	**Day 20**
Final revisions	Edit	Publish	"Dear Reader" letter	Celebrate

Appendix B

Mini-Lesson Template

Unit of Study focus: _____

Today's teaching point: _____

Text to use (mentor, teacher's, student's): _____

_____

Connect:

Activate their minds by briefly reviewing where you are in the unit of study, what you did yesterday, and what the next step is today.	"Writers, we've been working on . . ." "Today we will . . ."

Teach:

The teaching point is the next logical step in the unit, which typically builds on yesterday's lesson and supports tomorrow's lesson.	"Writers, let's look at how this author/student wrote his/her piece using X." or "Writers, watch how I do X in my writing."

Active Involvement:

Have students briefly try what you've taught in their notebooks or drafts. or Have them repeat what you've taught to a partner.	"Writers, please look at your writing and think about how this craft/strategy/process might work for you." or "Writers, please turn to your neighbor and explain the lesson's writing craft/strategy/process." "Who will try this today?" [*Wait for many hands.*]

Link and Excuse:

Link the work they'll be trying to closure. Explain how they will be sharing.	"Writers, at closure we'll share the work we've done today to help each other learn more. If you know what to do, look at me, and I'll excuse you."

Closure:

Share either the writing or the process. Share struggles and celebrate successes.	"Writers, you've all worked so hard today. Let's share how it went/your writing so we can learn more from each other."

Appendix C

Conference Guidance

Use a conversational tone, writer to writer. Five to eight minutes.

Opener	
Say the same opener every time.	"How's it going?"

Compliment	
Now or later. Point out something the student is doing well, label it with a character trait: commitment, discipline. Especially with struggling students, ask how they did a particular thing so they can articulate and internalize these positive actions.	"I see you got started right away. You are showing the discipline that good writers have. How did you do that?" "I see by what you have done here that you are applying the mini-lessons to improve your writing. You are showing the commitment that good writers have. How did you do that?"

Research	
Ask questions to help you understand what the student is thinking. Keep asking until you get a clear idea. Repeating whatever the child says lets him or her know you are really listening with interest and helps encourage the child to try to articulate his or her thinking.	"What are you working on?" "What are you trying to do in this part?" "Are you using a chart to help you today? Which one?" "Have you used a mentor text? Show me the part(s) you have used."

Decide	
Of all the things you could teach this child, what *one* thing would be of the most benefit? I actually say this aloud. It helps me keep the conference on track.	"I am trying to decide what writer's strategy would most benefit you and your work right now."

Appendix C (continued)

Teach

The number of strategies that you can choose to teach from will grow over time. Be patient. Your students are thrilled to have a one-on-one with you. Whatever you teach, phrase it globally. You are not here to correct the writing, you are here to teach the writer in a way that makes him or her more independent, not less. Occasionally, you won't know what to teach—give yourself extra time, ask other teachers, look at mentor texts.	"One strategy writers use when they don't know how to write their idea is first to talk out loud. You can do that with a partner or just yourself, or with me right now. Then you can write down what you heard yourself say." "When writers get stuck, they look at good writing to help them. Let's look at a mentor text together to see how (author) did what you are trying to do." "I am really not sure what to teach you right now. Let me think more about it, and I'll get back to you in 24 hours."

Interruption

Not allowed.	Without looking at the offender, hold up your palm in his/her direction. Continue conference.

Check for Understanding and Close

I never promise to check back later, because I get too busy elsewhere.	"Tell me what you will be doing now . . . I know you'll be able to continue this work on your own because you work hard, are so smart and are such a good writer."

Conference Assessment Sheet

What's done well	What's needed	Conventions

Appendix E

Comments to the Writer

Title: _____

Author: _____

Date: _____

Appendix F

Scoring Rubric

Element	⭑ ⭑ ⭑	⭑ ⭑	⭑
Meaning	Meaning is clear to the reader	Meaning is somewhat clear to the reader	Meaning is not clear to the reader
Structure	Structure is present and helps the reader	Structure is attempted	Confusing structure or no apparent structure
Detail	Purposeful sensory details pull the reader into the piece	Attempt at purposeful use of sensory details, sometimes distracting or not present	Minimal or haphazard use of sensory details
Pacing	Sentence structure, detail, and word choices purposefully slow or speed the pace to enhance the reader's experience	Attempt at controlling the pace through varied sentence structure and word choice	Limited or distracting attempt at using pacing strategies
Conventions			
Ending Punctuation	Provides a smooth read	Sporadically used ending punctuation	Ending punctuation is missing or rare
Spelling	High-frequency words are spelled correctly, other errors are not distracting	Most high-frequency words spelled correctly	Reader has difficulty deciphering many words in the piece
Capitalization	Capitalization rules are correctly applied	Capitalization rules are attempted	Capitalization is missing and/or caps are used randomly
Subtotal			

Name: _____ Date: _____ Score: _____

Children's Literature Cited

Bourgeois, P. (2003). *Oma's quilt*. Toronto, ON: Kids Can Press.

Dahl, R. (2007). *Fantastic Mr. Fox*. New York: Puffin.

Fox, M. (1995). *Wilfrid Gordon McDonald Partridge*. La Jolla, CA: Kane/Miller.

Frazee, M. (2003) *Roller coaster*. New York: Harcourt Children's Books.

Hesse, K. (2000). *Come on, rain!* New York: Scholastic.

MacLachlan, P. (1998). *What you know first*. New York: HarperTrophy.

Park, B. (1998). *Junie B. Jones and the stupid smelly bus*. New York: Scholastic.

Pérez, A. I. (2000). *My very own room/Mi propio cuartito*. San Francisco: Children's Book Press.

Polacco, P. (1990). *Thunder cake*. New York: Philomel.

Polacco, P. (1998). *My rotten redheaded older brother*. New York: Aladdin.

Ryan, P. M. (2003). *Hello ocean: Hola mar*. Watertown, MD: Charlesbridge.

Ryder, J. (1994). *My father's hands*. New York: HarperCollins.

Rylant, C. (1991). *Night in the country*. New York: Aladdin.

Rylant, C. (1993). *When I was young in the mountains*. New York: Puffin.

Schwartz, D. (1999). *If you hopped like a frog*. New York: Scholastic.

Smith, C. R., Jr. (2000). *Rimshots: Basketball pix, rolls, and rhythms*. New York: Puffin.

Williams, V. B. (1993). *A chair for my mother*. New York: HarperTrophy.

Yolen, J. (1987). *Owl moon*. New York: Philomel.

Yolen, J. (1997). *Welcome to the greenhouse*. New York: Putnam.

Yolen, J. (2000). *How do dinosaurs say goodnight?* New York: Blue Sky Press.

Yolen, J. (2003). *Least things: Poems about small natures*. Honesdale, PA: Boyds Mills Press.

Yolen, J. (2003). *Wild wings: Poems for young people*. Honesdale, PA: Boyds Mills Press.

Zolotow, C. (1985). *William's doll*. New York: HarperTrophy.

References

Anderson, C. (2000). *How's it going? A practical guide to conferring with student writers.* Portsmouth, NH: Heinemann.

Anderson, C. (2005). *Assessing writers.* Portsmouth, NH: Heinemann.

Angelillo, J. (2002). *A fresh approach to teaching punctuation.* New York: Scholastic.

Atwell, N. (1998). *In the middle: New understandings about writing, reading, and learning* (2nd ed.). Portsmouth, NH: Heinemann.

Calkins, L. M. (2007). *Units of study for teaching writing, grades 3–5.* Portsmouth, NH: Heinemann First Hand.

Chang, M. L. (2004). *Classroom management in photographs.* New York: Scholastic.

Heard, G. (1998). *Awakening the heart: Exploring poetry in elementary and middle school.* Portsmouth, NH: Heinemann.

Leograndis, D. (2006). *Fluent writing: How to teach the art of pacing.* Portsmouth, NH: Heinemann.

Marten, C. (2003). *Word crafting: Teaching spelling, grades K–6.* Portsmouth, NH: Heinemann.

Sitton, R., & Forest, R. G. (1986). *The Quick-Word handbook for everyday writers.* North Billerica, MA: Curriculum Associates.

Yolen, J. (2006). *Take joy: A writer's guide to loving the craft.* Cincinnati: Writer's Digest Books.

About the Author

Denise Leograndis is a full-time elementary school teacher for the Santa Clara Unified School District in the San Francisco Bay area. She is also a professional developer for her district and the Franklin–McKinley School District, where she and her colleagues plan and lead summer writing institutes. She is a guest lecturer for preservice and master's literacy classes at San Jose State University.

Denise lives in Sunnyvale with her husband of 26 years and their teenage son, one dog, and a rabbit. She loves snowshoeing in the Sierra Mountains and scuba diving anytime anywhere. But mostly she loves to teach.